CAM TRIBOLET

DEAD 13 TIMES

WHITAKER
HOUSE

What Others Are Saying About Cam Tribolet and *Dead 13 Times*...

I am really excited about Cam's story being published as a book. It has been my privilege to serve with him on The Way Outfitters board of directors and to share in support of physically disabled youth and veterans. Cam's story is amazing. He has overcome tremendous personal challenges and has been an inspiration to hundreds of people, and there is no doubt that this book will serve as an inspiration to thousands more.

—*John Gillespie*
Founder, Rawhide Boys Ranch
New London, Wisconsin

Cam Tribolet's story of perseverance in response to nearly unimaginable challenges is truly inspiring. He offers creative and practical advice for all of us who have ever doubted ourselves or our ability to make significant changes. After reading *Dead 13 Times*, you'll promise yourself not to make any more excuses and to live each and every day to the fullest.

—*Chuck Runyon*
CEO and cofounder, Anytime Fitness

Cam is one of the most inspirational people I have ever come across. The way he has handled adversity throughout his life is truly mind-blowing. Most people would have given up and felt sorry for themselves in the midst of such trying times. Cam's attitude, dedication, and drive are some of the attributes that I can hope to show my kids someday. I am forever changed after reading his story. I respect the way he lives his life and affects everyone in a positive manner. Cam's life should make us all want to make the best out of any situation we are in.

—*A.J. Hawk*
Linebacker, Green Bay Packers

CAM TRIBOLET

DEAD 13 TIMES

WHITAKER
HOUSE

The author is represented by MacGregor Literary, Inc., of Hillsboro, Oregon.

DEAD 13 TIMES:
LEARNING TO LIVE AFTER DYING

Cam Tribolet
ctribolet@frontier.com

ISBN: 978-1-60374-956-5
eBook ISBN: 978-1-60374-980-0
Printed in the United States of America
© 2014 by Cam Tribolet

Whitaker House
1030 Hunt Valley Circle
New Kensington, PA 15068
www.whitakerhouse.com

Library of Congress Cataloging-in-Publication Data (pending)

1 2 3 4 5 6 7 8 9 10 11 ⅏ 20 19 18 17 16 15 14

CONTENTS

ONE

SECOND CHANCES

f I hurry, I can still make the last call, I thought. I pulled out my keys from my pocket, popped the top on a beer, left the strip club, and got into my truck, determined to find a bar still open. This summer night in 1986 was just like any other night. I had settled into a routine that I liked—waking up at 5 AM, working at my construction job all day, coming home and showering, heading to the strip club, finishing the night at a bar, and then driving home and sleeping a few hours with my fiancée before starting it all over again. I'd been living that way since I'd graduated high school and moved out on my own. It was all I knew, and it seemed like the perfect lifestyle for a strong, healthy, independent twenty-three-year-old guy. Growing up, my dad had instilled in me that I needed to work hard if I ever planned to have anything in life. I took my dad's words to heart, and I worked hard to support my drug and alcohol habits. I worked hard and I partied hard.

Driving through Fort Wayne, Indiana, about three in the morning, I stopped at a red light and glanced at the four-door blue car next to me in the turn lane. I made eye contact with one of the three male passengers and gave him the customary head nod before looking back at the stoplight. The light was red for what seemed like a lifetime. Just then, one of the men got out of the car and walked over to my truck. I rolled down the window to see what he wanted, and his fist met my face. He punched me over and over and over again. As I tried to escape, he pulled out a gun and shot me three times in the stomach. I don't remember much of what happened next, but I somehow managed to escape. I tried to drive myself to the closest hospital, but after only a few blocks, I passed out, lost control of my truck, crossed the center line, and plowed through a fence behind a nearby bar, which was just about to close. My truck landed underneath a bunch of sewer pipes before coming to a stop. Hearing the loud noise, people from inside the bar rushed out to find me unconscious in my truck. Minutes later, I was at St. Joseph's Hospital, undergoing emergency surgery.

One bullet had pierced my aorta. Another had punctured my bowel. And the last bullet had torn through my intestines and lodged in my back. Because my bowel had spilled out into my body, I was full of infection. I remember hearing one of the doctors say, "No one survives with this much infection."

Shortly after, I went into cardiac arrest. That was the first time I died. Immediately, I had a vision—it was more real than a dream. I was replacing a windowsill—something I often did, working construction—and I remember thinking how rotten the sill was and how I needed to remove it. As I removed the sill, a bright light shot out at me from the wall. Just then, someone or something pushed me from behind, trying to get me to go into the wall, toward the light. But I didn't want to go; I held on to the side of the wall, using all my strength to stay put and not move toward the light.

As I was fighting for my life, one of the doctors on call was in the waiting room, breaking the news to my parents.

"We don't expect him to make it," the doctor told them. "We're doing all we can to stabilize him, but he continues to code…it doesn't look good."

The doctors resuscitated me, and I returned to my body—but not for long. They repaired my aorta with an aortic graft, but it soon failed due to the amount of infection in my body from my ruptured bowel. I died for a second time. And this time, I had a different vision. I was a movie actor coming out of my trailer, ready to perform my assigned scene. As I approached the director, he was mumbling something about the script.

"What are you talking about?" I asked.

"I'm talking about the light," he said, pointing to the script in his hand. "It says right here that you're supposed to go into the light."

"Well, I don't care what it says in that script," I hollered. "I'm not going into that light. I don't feel good about it!"

With that, I walked away from the director and away from the light. As I entered my trailer, I reentered my body. I was alive again. The doctors were putting in a new graft through my neck, but it was too late. Because of the severe loss of blood and the amount of infection streaming through my body, both of my legs developed gangrene. They had to be amputated above the knees, though I was unaware of it at the time. In addition, the doctors performed a tracheotomy to keep me breathing and installed a pacemaker to keep my heart going. But my body continued to shut down. One by one, my organs stopped functioning. As they did, I looked up at the numbers on the machine next to my bed, and they were all declining quickly. Alarms started going off all around me, and people were rushing around, calling out orders to one another.

"Stay with us, Cam," one of the nurses said, "stay with us."

I wanted to stay, but my bed started moving into the wall behind us, and all of the medical personnel started fading away from my vision. Suddenly, I heard my buddies' voices all around me: "How have you been?" "Man, it's been a long time." Next thing I knew, I was above my bed, looking down.

Why am I up here and my body's down there? I thought.

Everything became pitch-black, and I felt myself rising higher and higher, farther away from my body. I was screaming but not making a sound.

Just then, I heard, "Pow, pow, pow!"

Am I being shot at again?

I learned later that I was being shocked back to life. As the paddles restarted my heart, I returned to my body.

"He's back," someone said.

I wondered for how long. The doctors had done all they could do. I wasn't expected to live through the night.

The In-between

While I hovered somewhere between life and death, Mom and Dad went to the funeral home to start making arrangements. I knew I was dying, and yet I wasn't particularly afraid. I saw that familiar, intense light, but this time, I also saw Jesus reaching out for me. I knew it was Jesus, even though I'd never given Him much attention in my twenty-three years on earth. I'd always heard stories of people dying and "seeing the light," but my family had never gone to church, so I knew absolutely nothing about the concept of being saved. I guess I'd always believed there was a heaven and a hell, but I'd never thought about where I might spend eternity.

Suddenly, I felt the warmth and peace of that bright light. Then that warm and peaceful sensation lifted from me, and I was enveloped by cold and emptiness. When I looked up, I was looking right into the face of the devil. He was hideous, and I knew he wanted me. It felt like I was in an after-life tug-of-war. I was witnessing firsthand the struggle of good versus evil, and I was the prize. At that moment, I knew the devil had an eternity of pain and torture planned for me, and I panicked! I was fighting hard, trying with everything in me to get back to the light, back to heaven, back to Jesus. But I couldn't. I couldn't get there. Then I was jarred back into my body. I had been resuscitated once again. I heard voices of family members and medical personnel all around, so I knew I was back, but I didn't know for how long. Minutes later, I coded again. This time, I saw a crucifix on the wall—a common sight at St. Joe's. It was a Catholic hospital, after all. I didn't know if my eyes were open or if I was dreaming, but I focused on Jesus, hanging on that cross, and then I was amazed when He got off the cross and came toward me.

Am I dying? Am I already dead? Is He coming to take me to heaven? I thought.

Just as I was about to take His hand and go with Him, Jesus turned into a demonic monster. I screamed—if not out loud, at least on the inside—trying to utter the name of Jesus. When I did, I was back again. I could hear my family talking about me.

"He's not going to make it, is he?" my mom said, her voice cracking.

I heard my fiancée crying.

One by one, my relatives said good-bye to me. I had never been close with my family, so it was odd to hear each person speaking so kindly to me. My fiancée and her parents said their good-byes, too, and I wanted to tell them, "I am still alive. I'm coming out of this. Don't give up on me!"

On the very night that everyone expected me to die, my kidneys started working again. I was given a second chance—a chance to get it right this time— but I had no idea what awaited me when I awoke.

Waking Up to a Nightmare

My feet really hurt, I thought, as my eyes fluttered open for the first time in weeks. I saw a nurse nearby, so I tried to tell her about the pain in my feet, but I couldn't speak. I groaned to get her attention.

"You had to have a tracheotomy, Mr. Tribolet," the nurse stated very matter-of-factly. "Don't try to speak."

With that, she handed me a pen and paper, explaining that I had been in an accident and was currently receiving treatment in a hospital. I couldn't remember much of anything that had transpired.

"Write it," she instructed me.

I scribbled as best I could, "My feet hurt!"

The nurse read my words and said very bluntly, "Your feet can't hurt, Mr. Tribolet. You don't have any legs."

Immediately I looked down at my legs, which were covered by a blanket, and I could tell that part of me was missing. I had to be restrained. Many emotions shot through my body; fear, anger, bitterness, and disbelief overwhelmed me. I hoped I was dreaming, but I knew I wasn't.

The next few weeks were filled with lots of poking and prodding, and lots of painkillers and frequent visits from friends and family. My father, who had broken both legs in a work accident right before my ordeal, rolled in on his wheelchair to see me every day. We were quite a pair. Still, it was nice to have him—or anyone, for that matter—come to see me. After my mom learned I was going to live, she stopped coming to see me. She was busy working as a unit clerk in a different hospital down the street, and said she'd come to visit when she had some downtime. Apparently, that downtime never came. But at least I had my dad— which was odd, because we'd never had a good relationship in the past. And, of course, I had my fiancée and her parents.

Suffering from pneumonia and bedsores, in addition to all of my other injuries, I was an absolute mess. Because of the damage to my bowel, I was fed by a tube and was given an ileostomy bag while my bowel healed. This open wound required frequent cleanings, and every time the nurses came to do it, they would have to shoot me up with morphine so that I could endure the literal scrubbing of my insides. The pain was so intense, I thought I would die. Every day seemed like the last—more tests, more suctioning, more blood work, more wound cleaning, more excruciating pain. I lived for the next friendly visit or the next phone call, but not every visit turned out to be so friendly. My fiancée wasn't visiting as often as she had been, and I assumed she was just busy. My assumptions were wrong. She breezed into the hospital room one evening, and I smiled at the scent of her perfume. It was so good to see her. But she didn't smile back at me.

"What's wrong?" I scribbled on my notepad.

She didn't say anything for several minutes, and then she took off her engagement ring and placed it on the side table next to my hospital bed. I looked up at her with tears in my eyes.

Surely I haven't lost her, too....

But my thoughts were interrupted by her words—words that my mind would replay over and over again as I came to terms with my new life.

"Cam," she said, without looking at me or touching me, "I just don't think I can marry a man with no legs...I'm sorry."

And with that monotone statement, she walked out of my hospital room and out of my life. I had survived the shooting and numerous surgeries, including the amputation of my legs, but I wasn't sure I could survive this latest trial. I had lost so much—my legs, my fiancée, my livelihood, my independence, and my home. I had lost all hope. I decided that very night what my next move would be. As soon as I was released from the hospital, I would take my own life, or the little that was left of it.

TWO

A REASON TO LIVE

Days turned into weeks, and weeks turned into months, and I was still in the hospital. I was making progress physically, but I was dead on the inside. I had put the concerns of my past and future out of my mind. I couldn't deal with all of that—at least not now. The only reason I wanted to get better at that time was so that I could go home and end my life—in my own way, on my own terms. Little did I know that God had other plans for me.

After six months of recovery at Saint Joseph's Hospital, my feeding tube was removed. I had to relearn how to eat. At six feet two, I was down to only 133 pounds, so the doctors really wanted me to put on some weight. In fact, no meal request was too outrageous. If I said I was craving a Big Mac and a chocolate milkshake from McDonald's, that's what I was served. My job was to keep the food down, which proved to be more difficult than expected.

Not only was I relearning how to eat, but the six-month mark since I'd entered the hospital came with another challenge—receiving my artificial legs. Yes, it was a medical milestone, but I was less than enthused to receive them or try to use them. I had pretty much given up on everything, but I hid my feelings from my family and the medical staff, and simply tried to be a good patient. If they wanted me to begin rehabilitation and learn how to use my new legs, I would go through the motions—anything to get out of the hospital sooner.

"Are you ready for rehab?" one of the nurses asked.

I nodded affirmatively. However, I was so weak that I wasn't sure if I could even sit up. That was my first obstacle to overcome. After all, I'd been lying in a hospital bed for six months. After only a few moments in the rehab room, the nurses sat me up, and I immediately felt sick. Just then, one of the physical therapists ran over to help me.

She is beautiful, I thought, as I looked up from the puke pan that she held for me.

I'd never seen her at the hospital before. Suddenly, therapy didn't seem like such a bad idea. No matter how painful it was, if it meant getting to see the hot therapist on a regular basis, I was game.

So I convinced my orthopedic doctor to prescribe myofascial release therapy for my pain. He ordered weekly therapy with a rehab therapist named Mindy and her assistant—the beautiful woman who had held my puke pan. I definitely wanted to get to know her better. The next week, we began meeting—just the three of us.

"Hi, Cam. Looks like we're going to be working together the next few weeks," Mindy said. "And Sue is going to be assisting in your therapy."

I smiled at Sue, trying to be cool, but I felt ridiculous. It wasn't like I was on my game, in a bar, hitting on a hot girl. I was in a hospital gown, with tubes and hoses sticking out of me, jaundiced beyond belief, and ready to throw up at any moment. Yeah, I was a real catch. Still, she didn't seem to mind all of my drawbacks. Conversation came easy between us. At first, we chatted about insignificant things—the weather, sports, hospital food—but as the weeks continued, our conversations deepened.

I eventually felt comfortable enough to tell her about my recent breakup, and how I'd lost pretty much everything in my life since the shooting. Somehow, she knew just what to say, making me feel like less of a loser. She didn't feel sorry for me or pity me. She treated me like a man, and I sensed that she cared for me. I could see it in her eyes and in the way she smiled at me when I rolled into therapy each week. She actually seemed happy to see me. As an outpatient therapist, Sue wasn't at the hospital all the time, so I took advantage of our minutes together during my sessions.

After about a month of weekly therapy sessions with Sue, I got up enough courage to ask her the question I'd been longing to pose for several weeks.

"So, um, do you have a boyfriend?" I asked, searching her eyes for the answer.

"Not at the moment," she said, with just a hint of a smile.

It was the first time I'd felt true happiness since awakening from my coma. I had a glimmer of hope that my life wasn't over, and a glimmer was enough to keep me pushing on. I took a risk and sent Sue flowers, hoping that she liked me as much as I liked her.

After eight months of recovery, I was released from the hospital into my parents' care in April 1987. After living on my own for more than four years, I was now forced to move back in with Mom and Dad. It was humiliating, depressing, confining, and miserable. But I did have regular outpatient therapy sessions with Sue, and that gave me something to look forward to each week.

One day during our weekly therapy session, Sue just looked at me with her amazing eyes and said, "Well, if you're not going to ask me out, I guess I'll have to ask you."

At first, I wasn't sure I'd heard her correctly. *Why would she want to go out with me?* I asked myself. *I literally have nothing to offer her.*

In the most flirtatious tone I could muster, I asked, "Are you asking me out?"

"I guess I am," she flirted back.

"In that case, where are you taking me?" I countered.

"How about if I make you dinner at my place?"

This just keeps getting better and better, I thought.

So, that Friday night, Sue picked me up at my mom and dad's house, drove me to her place, and served me a delicious dinner. We talked for hours about everything and nothing. I felt as if I'd known her my whole life, but I was glad I hadn't, because I was pretty sure she wouldn't have liked the old Cam—the Cam who partied all the time, cheated on his girlfriend, and never would have measured up to this good Catholic girl's standards. I knew that if the relationship was going to have a shot, I would need to quit using drugs and stop feeling sorry for myself. The problem was, I didn't know if I could do either. After being weaned off morphine from my eight-month hospital stay, I had secretly started using cocaine. It helped with both my physical and emotional pain, and it got me through the periods when I couldn't see Sue. Since I was sort of dating her, I'd had to get a different therapist, so I no longer saw her for regular therapy sessions.

I thought about Sue all the time—the way she smelled, the way she laughed, the way her eyes lit up when she talked about her love of children. I was falling for her, and that scared me. I didn't want to get hurt again, and I also couldn't see what I had to offer her.

One day, while watching TV at my parents' house, I was feeling sorry for myself again, thinking about how much money I had made working construction, when a commercial caught my attention.

"Going nowhere?"

Yes.

"In a dead-end job?"

I don't even have a job.

"Would you like to have the education to help you secure your dream job?"

Yes, I think I would.

"Then make this life-changing call like I did. Call ITT Tech and put yourself on the right path today!"

As if the girl in the commercial was controlling my actions, I picked up the phone and dialed the number. Minutes later, I was on the "right path" and pursuing a degree in architectural engineering. It might not have been a big step in the world's eyes, but it was monumental for me. I felt like I was back in the game again.

Shutting Up and Stepping Out

Sue had given me something to live for, but I wasn't sure how to live in my new body. More than anything, I wanted to be independent, and the first step toward regaining my independence was getting my car altered so that I could drive again. It didn't take me long to have hand controls installed in my car and a wheel chair ramp built at my parents' house—two huge accomplishments. Sue had become much more important to me than drugs, so I quit doing cocaine cold turkey. I craved her love and approval more than I wanted to get high.

Sue and I had been dating for several weeks, and I still hadn't kissed her. I wanted to take her in my arms and let her know how much I loved her, but I just couldn't work up enough courage to make them move.

What if she rejects me? I thought. *What if she is just being nice to me because she feels sorry for me?*

It had been an emotional day already. Mom had taken me down to the police station so that I could watch the video of the accident site and begin to piece together what had actually happened to me. Seeing the graphic footage on the crime scene video reawakened details of that horrible night—details I had blocked out for a reason. I felt like I was being shot at all over again. I gripped the arms of my wheelchair so hard that my knuckles turned white. Memories of the worst night of my life flooded my senses. Finally, I just couldn't watch another minute. I didn't want to know any more than I already did. I dropped Mom off at home and headed for Sue's apartment. I needed to see my girlfriend.

As I arrived at her apartment complex, I was overcome with emotion. I just sat there, unable to pull myself together enough to go inside. I determined that I would find out that night if her feelings were real or if I was falling in love all by myself. I wheeled myself into her apartment, and she greeted me with her sweet smile.

"What's wrong?" she asked, obviously aware I'd been crying.

"I have to ask you something, and I want you to be brutally honest," I said.

"OK," she said, sitting down in a chair next to me.

"Why would you ever want to be with a man like me?" I asked, trying to keep it together. "I mean, could you really ever love me?"

Sue grabbed my face in her hands, looked me straight in the eyes, and said, "Shut up and kiss me."

I had my answer.

She loved me, even though I had nothing much to offer, and that made me want to become a better man. After that kiss, I knew I would one day ask her to marry me. I just had to make some changes in my life first. The more time I spent with Sue, the happier I was, and the more confident I became.

Meet the Parents

Sue and I were officially an item, which meant I had to meet her family. I was nervous; I didn't know what they would think of me, but it was time to find out. During dinner together, I made a point of telling her parents about my pursuit of an architectural engineering degree, as well as my plans of becoming Catholic. After all, Sue came from a family of devout Catholics, while my family had no religion at all, and I knew that if I wanted to marry her, I would have to join the Catholic Church. It only made sense to start down the road to Catholicism and earn some brownie points with Sue's parents along the way. I knew in my heart that I should take her father aside after dinner and ask for Sue's hand in marriage, but I just couldn't. I wanted to, but I just couldn't bring myself to utter those words, out of fear he might not give us his blessing. Still, I knew I would eventually ask Sue to marry me, and I knew it would be sooner than later. I wasn't about to let her get away.

I sold the engagement ring that my former fiancée had returned to me, then used that money, along with some I had managed to save, to buy a ring Sue could be proud of.

At that point, I had the ring; I just didn't know if I had the courage to actually ask her to marry me. Out of breath and flushed, I wheeled into her apartment and made small talk as she tidied up in the kitchen. When she finally came into the living room, I was all teeth, grinning from ear to ear. She had to know I was up to something.

I didn't know if my proposal would go down in history as one of the most romantic, but I knew it would at least be unique.

"Sue, you know I love you."

"Yes, of course," she answered.

"I can't imagine my life without you in it," I continued, and then I grabbed her ring, which I had hidden inside one of my artificial legs.

She smiled and bit her bottom lip, as she always did when she was nervous.

"So, I was wondering if you would do me the great honor of becoming my wife."

She had tears in her eyes. I hoped that was a good sign. She hugged me and whispered "Yes" in my ear while we were still embracing. After I put the ring on her finger, I felt like the luckiest man alive. Not only had I died thirteen times and survived, but I'd been given a beautiful woman to share my new life with. That was more than I thought I deserved.

Gaining Ground

With Sue in my life, I had gained so much confidence that I was actually pursuing the things I used to love once again. After I had built my own wheelchair ramp at my parents' house, I started constructing wheelchair ramps for other people, to make a little money on the side. On one particular job, the homeowner rolled out in his wheelchair, looked at me in my own wheelchair, and shook his head.

"Makes me feel kind of guilty," he mumbled, "having someone in my same situation build a ramp for me."

"No worries," I said. "I was in the construction business before I was in a wheelchair, so I can still build just about anything."

"Good to know," he said. "Can you play basketball?"

"Well, I could before this," I said, gesturing to my lack of legs. "I used to be six foot two, with a pretty good jump shot."

"We could use a guy like you on our team," he said, then proceeded to tell me all about the wheelchair basketball league he played in twice a week.

"Sounds like fun," I agreed. "I'm in!"

Not only was I enjoying a little construction work, earning my degree from ITT Tech, and playing in a wheelchair basketball league, but I was also contemplating trying things I'd never thought I would do again, like hunting. In fact, I had sold all of my guns and hunting gear when I'd returned home from the hospital, sure that I'd never be able to hunt again, but my future brother-in-law, Bobbie, said I should reconsider. An avid hunter, he was quickly becoming my best friend. I told him I'd think about it. But first, I had another goal I wanted to achieve, and I was pretty sure it was going to take all of my free time to reach it.

Learning to Walk Again

As a double above-the-knee amputee, I knew my chances of being able to walk again were not good. The words of my orthopedic doctor played over and over again in my head. "Get used to being in a wheelchair," he'd told me a few months into my therapy. "Double above-the-knee amputees typically do not learn to walk on artificial limbs. They usually give up, due to how hard it is."

I had tried not to dwell on his diagnosis or his discouraging words, because I knew that I was capable of accomplishing more than anyone thought I could. That's the way I'd always been, and I wasn't about to change now. I wanted to marry Sue, and I wanted to walk her down the aisle, not be pushed along beside her.

Secretly, I turned to Sue's therapist friend Flo Webb, who lived an hour from us, in hopes that she could help me learn to walk on my artificial legs in time for our wedding. With the wedding date only six months off, I knew had my work cut out for me, but I also knew I was in good hands. Flo had worked with WWII veterans and knew exactly how to help me. Every day, without Sue's knowledge, I worked toward my goal of walking on my own.

I had to learn to navigate all different types of terrain—pavement, gravel, dirt, grass, hardwood, and so on. It was exhausting, but I was getting stronger every day. As I balanced myself on my crutches one February day, Flo coached from the sidelines.

"You can do this," she encouraged me. "Make sure where you place your crutch is stable when switching from one kind of terrain to another."

I went from pavement to dirt and back several times without much trouble.

"Nice," she said, then paused. "So, do you think you're ready to move from the crutches to the canes?"

I stared down at my artificial legs, then looked back up at Flo. "I think the real question is, do you think I'm ready?"

She nodded yes, so I agreed to begin working with canes at our next session.

There were bumps and bruises along the way. There were times I wanted to quit. But something inside me kept driving me, pushing me to succeed. I went from a wheelchair to a walker to crutches. My goal was to walk Sue down the aisle with only two canes. I couldn't wait to surprise her.

THREE

A WALK OF LOVE

Since we'd decided on a Catholic wedding, we had to meet with the priest for premarital counseling and to settle the details of the ceremony. I wasn't worried about the premarital counseling, because I loved Sue so much it hurt, and I knew we were meant to be together. However, the ceremony details made me a little uneasy. As we discussed them, it became clear that our wedding was going to be lengthy, and I wasn't sure I'd be able to stand the whole time.

"Why don't we have a chair up front for you to sit in if you get tired?" the priest suggested.

"No, I don't want that," I said.

"Why not, honey?" Sue asked, grabbing my hand. "It's going to be a long day."

"No, I want to *stand* by you—not *sit* by you. Besides, you're too pretty to stand up there alone," I added. This was her special day, and I didn't want to ruin it or take the focus off of my beautiful bride. I was determined to stand for the entire ceremony and then walk her back down the aisle using only two canes.

Though I had been working with Flo for several months, I didn't graduate to two canes by myself until two days before the big day—March 5, 1988.

"You can do this!" Flo encouraged me, as I practiced walking with my canes on a carpeted area one last time.

I just smiled, proud of myself for accomplishing what I'd set out to do. I couldn't wait to surprise Sue. She had no idea I had been planning to walk her back down the aisle.

On the day of the wedding, I was nervous, excited, happy, and overwhelmed, but mostly nervous. I was thankful to have all my guys around me—my four groomsmen, which consisted of two work friends, my brother Tracey, and my future brother-in-law, Bobbie. As I put on my patent leather shoes, I realized that I hadn't worn a tux since my senior prom, seven years prior. And then it hit me. *Oh, no. I haven't practiced walking with my canes in patent leather shoes. I've always been in Reeboks!*

I was grateful that Sue was getting ready with her bridesmaids in another part of the church, out of earshot of my heightening nerves.

"It's time," I heard someone say from the hallway.

I took a deep breath and headed for the sanctuary. As I walked out front with my groomsmen, I saw the runner stretched down the long aisle.

Great, I thought. *I practiced on carpeting but never on a runner.*

Just then, I looked around at the wedding guests and made eye contact with Flo, who was smiling from ear to ear. She had confidence in me, and that gave me the courage I needed to conquer my fears of the patent leather shoes and the wedding runner that awaited me after the vows. Then the music began, and I gazed down the aisle, past the bunch of hot-pink bridesmaids, and locked eyes with the woman of my dreams. Sue was more beautiful than any bride had ever been—I was sure of it. We exchanged the traditional vows, and I meant every word of them. We lit the unity candle, and I prevailed as the hero, keeping Sue's veil from catching on fire. That bit of humor sort of lightened the formality of the ceremony, and I sailed through the rest of it. I don't remember all of the particulars, but I do remember the moment when the priest said, "You may now kiss your bride."

I kissed Sue like I'd never kissed her before, and the hundreds of people who filled the church cheered for us. As we turned to go down the aisle, I smiled at Sue and began walking beside her. She immediately went into physical therapist mode and grabbed my arm with a firm grip, which just made me smile even more.

She had my back, and if I went down, she was going down with me. But I didn't fall. I made it to the receiving line and greeted all of our guests. Even the family of my ex-fiancée had come to celebrate my new life.

After the wedding pictures were finished, we climbed into a limousine and headed for Shiloh Reception Hall in Fort Wayne, Indiana. Though I was elated to finally be Sue's husband, I was physically spent. I wasn't used to wearing my artificial legs for more than a few hours a day, so I was exhausted, and we still had dinner and dancing ahead of us. Yet I was determined to enjoy every minute of this beautiful day. As I gazed at Sue, riding in the limo toward the reception hall, I just couldn't stop smiling. I couldn't believe that this amazing woman had married me—with no legs and no job and enough medical bills to wallpaper the church. She'd taken a leap of faith and chosen me. At that point in my life, I wasn't exactly on speaking terms with God. I had talked to Him a bit in the hospital after the accident, when I wasn't sure if I was going to live or even if I wanted to, but I was full of gratitude for what He had done. I knew it had taken some divine intervention for Sue to fall in love with a man like me, and I would be forever thankful.

The First Dance

When it was time for our first dance, I could barely stand, but I held Sue really tight, hoping I wouldn't fall. She didn't let me. As mushy as it sounds, when I was in her arms, I felt strength, and the pain I'd been feeling just moments before vanished completely. As we moved around the dance floor, I knew that everything I had been through was worth it. When we finished our dance, Flo came up to me and gave me a huge hug.

"You did it!" She was beaming.

"Yes, I did," I said, "and Sue was surprised. We did good."

As I was whisked away for the cutting of the cake, I mouthed the words "Thank you" to Flo. The rest of the afternoon flew by—the tossing of the bridal bouquet and the garter, the meal, more dancing, more visiting with guests. Even my family behaved themselves. So, all in all, our wedding day was the best I could've hoped for. Sue and I were the last to leave the reception hall. We were tired. My legs were swollen. But we were very excited about our honeymoon.

Bound for the Bahamas

It had been a weekend of firsts for me: First time to get married. First time to wear my artificial legs for more than a few hours. First time to go on vacation with Sue. And it was my first time to fly. I'm not embarrassed to admit that I was a little scared. But, as it turned out, our flight attendant was an old high school friend of mine, and she took good care of us.

When we exited the airport in Nassau, the warm weather greeted us. Our resort was everything we'd hoped it would be—even better than the brochure had made it sound.

I wanted our honeymoon to be picture-perfect, too, but there were a few things I couldn't accomplish. No matter how hard I tried, I wasn't able to walk on the sand with my legs. There would be no moonlit walks on the beach with my love. She'd have to settle for moonlit walks around the pool. And it was 1988, long before the ADA (Americans with Disabilities Act) was put into effect, so not everything in the hotel could accommodate those with mobility issues. Every outing was an obstacle course for me—curbs, stairs, and so on. But Sue helped me, and I didn't let the minor challenges ruin our wonderful time together. In fact, I didn't think anything could dampen my mood, but I was wrong. Our first day out by the pool, I noticed that everyone—literally every single person—was staring at me. Up until that time, the only people I had been around knew what had happened to me, so I hadn't had to deal with the constant staring and whispering—until now. I tried to play it cool and just bask in the sun next to my beautiful bride, but every time I opened my eyes, I was met with lots of other eyes that were all looking at me.

I leaned over and whispered in Sue's ear, "Everyone is staring."

"So?" she said, without even looking up. "Who cares?"

Her "it's no big deal" attitude helped me overcome my feelings of inferiority, and I decided that very moment that I would no longer allow the stares and whispers to detract from my vacation fun. I figured that if my wife didn't see me as a freak, why should I care if others did?

Dolphins, Sharks, and Big Fish Stories

The dolphin exhibit was right next to the pool, which was nice. I would put a beach towel over my legs, and Sue would wheel me down, right next to the dolphin pool. It was a relaxing week in paradise. We were able to talk and laugh and just enjoy each other...most of the time. At one point, I was lying in the sun with my eyes closed when I felt someone staring. I could actually feel someone's presence. Sure enough, when I opened my eyes, a little boy was standing right next to me. Before I could say anything to him, he blurted out, "What happened to your legs?"

Without missing a beat, I replied, "I was swimming in the ocean, and a shark ate them."

"Cam!" Sue scolded. "That's not true!"

The little boy's face went completely white, and big tears welled in his eyes.

"He's kidding," she consoled the little boy. "Cam, tell him you're kidding."

I was laughing too hard to say anything, but I am pretty sure that young man never went into the ocean the rest of his vacation. Even though I didn't win over any kids on that particular trip, Sue was confident I'd be a good father, and she told me so.

"I want four or five or maybe even six children," she said, rubbing more sunscreen on my scarred body.

"Six!" I said, peering over the top of my sunglasses. "That's a lot. How about two?"

"Let's start with two and then see how we feel," Sue compromised, grinning mischievously, because she knew she could probably talk me into anything—especially while wearing that bikini.

The talk of children—as many as six—prompted a discussion about our housing situation. We really weren't sure where to live, now that we were a married couple. Sue had her apartment, and I still had my bachelor pad of a trailer. In fact, it was the only thing I hadn't lost after the accident. But I knew it wasn't fit for a lady. It had sheets as curtains in the windows, and the best-looking item in the entire trailer was a bumper pool table.

"It's probably time to sell the bachelor pad," I admitted.

"Time to put it out of its misery," Sue joked.

I still had another year of school at ITT Tech, but my classes met for only half of the day, so I had managed to find work interning for an engineering firm. Sue had quit her job at St. Joe's Hospital to pursue a better opportunity at another hospital, and we figured that, with our two incomes, we could afford a starter house. Such big decisions were made poolside, while we sipped our tropical drinks and watched the dolphins dance and play. We were two twenty-five-year-olds with our whole lives ahead of us, and we couldn't have been happier. Every morning when I woke up with Sue in my arms, I was reminded of how lucky I was to have a second chance at life, and how blessed I was to have someone to share it with.

A Double Blessing

Marrying into Sue's family was a double blessing. Not only did I get the woman of my dreams, but I also got the family I'd always wanted. I became especially close to my brother-in-law, Bobbie. Whenever we were together, he would always talk hunting with me.

"You know, you should get a bow and start hunting with me this bow season," Bobbie said.

"I don't know," I said, looking over at Sue. "We both have student loans to pay off, and I really don't think I can afford to spend money on a bow right now."

"You're in luck," Bobbie continued, "because I know a guy who won a bow and is willing to part with it for seventy-five bucks."

"Really?"

"Really," he said. "Now what's your excuse?"

"Well, I've never hunted with a bow," I countered. "Who knows if I could even do it? I mean, I am in a wheelchair...how would I get around in the woods?"

"I'll help you," Bobbie assured me. "We'll figure something out."

"Well, I do have an uncle in Huntington with some land," I remembered, "and I think he has a three-wheeler. I might be able to use that to get around."

"You should buy the bow," Sue interjected. "Seriously, you know you want to get back into hunting. I've caught you watching hunting shows on TV several times since Bobbie first mentioned it to you. Just do it!"

"OK, I'll buy it," I finally conceded, a little nervous but also excited. "And when bow season comes around, maybe I'll be even stronger and better able to get around in the woods."

I was getting stronger and stronger every day at my job. As an inspector for the engineering firm, I had to walk around various construction sites every single day. I was using my canes and learning to navigate all types of terrain—from wooden planks to gravel—and I was becoming pretty steady on my prosthetic legs.

Maybe I will be able to bow hunt, I thought.

After work, I would spend time with Bobbie, practicing for bow season, which was just around the corner. And, to my surprise, I was becoming very proficient with the bow.

However, I soon discovered that target practice was quite different from hunting with a bow. The hunting trips didn't prove very productive for me. Bobbie shot a deer with his bow, but I was never able to get close enough. Even though Bobbie put brush all around the three-wheeler to camouflage it, the exhaust gave me away every time. However, gun season was coming up, and I was hopeful. Since the fumes from the three-wheeler were an automatic alert to the deer, I knew I had to somehow get into a tree stand in order to get my shot. So, Bobbie and I built a wooden ladder out of two-by-fours, and I practiced climbing into a deer stand. He was my spotter, placing my "foot" on a rung while I grabbed the tree and hugged it. One rung at a time, I inched my way up the tree and finally made it to the stand. It was a slow process, but the stronger I grew, the better I got at it.

Bobbie already had his deer for the season, so his hunting enthusiasm was waning. Still, he took me out most weekends. As gun season drew to a close, I wanted to go just one more time, and I wanted to go alone. So, I gave Bobbie the weekend off and headed out by myself. I wasn't sure if I would be able to get into the deer stand without Bobbie's help, but I figured that if I couldn't, I would just hunt from the ground.

That November morning was perfect. I rode the three-wheeler out to the tree with our makeshift ladder, and I carefully climbed the trunk until I finally pulled myself up and onto the tree stand. That, in itself, was an accomplishment, even if I didn't get a deer. But I still wanted a buck. It was so quiet that morning that I could actually hear the snowflakes falling all around me. Just as the sun was coming up, in all its orange splendor, a buck appeared within my range. Using my father's sixteen-gauge shotgun, I shot him. He dropped, and I smiled.

I slid down the tree, which was much easier than climbing it, and eased onto the three-wheeler to go see my deer. It was my first successful kill as a handicapped hunter, and I couldn't have been prouder. Later, my uncle helped me load my deer, and I drove it all the way to Bobbie's house. He celebrated with me, and together we cleaned and dressed my kill.

As I headed home that morning, I thought, *If I can do that, I can do anything.*

To commemorate such an important event, I had that deer head mounted. It was more than just a trophy—it was the beginning of a new life for me. Finally, I realized that my handicap didn't define me, and I was never going to let it keep me from doing anything again.

FOUR

STARTING A FAMILY

Although she was only twenty-five years old, Sue's biological clock was ticking so loudly that we could both hear it. She wanted to start a family immediately after returning from the honeymoon, and I reluctantly agreed. Sue had been raised in this *Leave It to Beaver* type of family, and I had been raised in pure hell. Her parents were still happily married; mine were still married but hated each other. Dad wouldn't divorce Mom because he didn't want to give her anything. Sue was very close to all five of her siblings; I had no relationship with my oldest brother and rarely spoke to my other two siblings. Sue had memories of family dinners every night, as well as family devotions and hugs before bedtime. As hard as I tried, I couldn't remember either of my parents ever saying "I love you" to each other, to my siblings, or to me. And the only time God was mentioned in our household was in the middle of a stream of curse words.

I had grown up in a home of drugs, dysfunction, abuse, and apathy. I honestly had no idea what a normal family looked like. I had started drinking at age ten to escape my horrible home life. Alcohol was easy to come by in my house because my parents owned a bar in town, so I could sneak drinks anytime I wished. Several alcohol distributors routinely gave Dad gifts, and he started collecting Jim Beam decanters. They were all over our house, and Dad never noticed if a little whiskey was gone. So, whether I was at the bar with Mom or at home with

Dad, I had easy access to alcohol. I don't know if Mom and Dad were aware I was drinking every day, but I figured if they did find out, they wouldn't care. Mom was usually doped up on Valium, and Dad stayed out late with his girlfriends most nights; my siblings and I basically parented ourselves. No one woke us up for school. Nobody made sure we had clean clothes to wear. No one packed our lunches, wrote our school notes, cared for us when we were sick, or showed up for school functions—even the mandatory ones. Deep down, I really wanted a different life, but I knew it was just a stupid dream that would never come true.

Every chance I got, I would hang out at a friend's house. His mom's name was Bev, and she was the June Cleaver type of mother—the type I'd always wanted. She would make my favorite dessert and ask me about my day. I liked her so much that I always talked about her when I came home, bragging about her cooking and telling my siblings how nice she was to me. Well, this didn't go over very well with my own mom, and she called Ms. Bev and told her that I would no longer be allowed to go to her house. I was crushed. Ms. Bev had been my one shot at experiencing a normal childhood.

Still, I tried desperately to make believe I had a different life. When my brothers and sister left for school each day, I'd act like I was going, too, but then I'd break into a neighbor's house after he'd left for work and watch TV all day long. Sitting on a normal family's couch, eating a normal family's snacks, watching a normal family's TV—that was so much better than going to school or staying home in my own mess of a house. Occasionally, I would steal money from the neighbors and use it to play video games at a nearby arcade. Immersing myself in the fantasy world of video games was just another way I could check out of my life for hours at a time. I never wanted to face reality, because it was too hard.

"Wouldn't it be great if I were pregnant by Christmas?" Sue interrupted my thoughts.

"What? Umm…yes," I said. "That would be great if you were pregnant by Christmas."

Christmas. That had never been a happy time at my house. Dad hated Christmas and told us so every year. We'd put up the Christmas tree, and he would walk past it and say, "That is so stupid. Take down that tree." There were never any gifts, no family holiday traditions—just more pain and fighting. I guess that's why I graduated from drinking alcohol to smoking pot to taking pills, all before I was in junior high. I could get speed and Quaaludes pretty easily at school, on the days I actually showed up.

"And if I did get pregnant before Christmas," Sue continued, "I'd be having the baby about the same time you finish your degree. It'd be perfect timing!"

I just nodded and smiled, trying to be encouraging to Sue and to be excited about the possibility of being a dad sometime in the near future. But, in all honesty, I wasn't excited at all. What if I were the kind of father my dad had been to me? I'll never forget the night Mom said I was just like him.

Sometimes, the combination of taking pills and drinking alcohol acted as a truth serum for my mom. When on a binge, she would usually tell it to me straight. One night, in particular, Mom had been drinking and taking pills, and her slurred statements hurt more than usual. I was sixteen at the time, muddling my way through high school and earning a modest living helping Dad in his construction business. Working with him was about the only time I saw him during that season, because he had moved into a downtown studio apartment he shared with his eighteen-year-old girlfriend. His departure had taken a toll on Mom, and her bender this particular evening was really bad. Realizing she was in a mood, I quickly walked past her and headed for my room. I didn't want to field any questions about my dad or his new life, but she grabbed my arm before I could get by.

"Hey," she said, peering up at me through squinty eyes and a haze of cigarette smoke.

"What do you need, Mom?" I asked.

As I listened to her rampage of curses, I figured she just needed to unload on someone, and I was the only person around. I didn't say a word; I just stood there and took it. When I thought she'd finally finished, I walked away and heard these words before I shut my bedroom door: "I hate you...you are just like your father."

What if she were right? What if I turned out to be the kind of man who never had a positive word to say to anyone—even his own children? What if I turned out to be the kind of dad who beat his kids? What if I became the father who didn't know how to love and therefore didn't love his children like a father should? What if...?

"Did you hear me?" Sue asked.

"Only part of it," I said. In reality, I hadn't heard a word of what she'd been saying.

"I said I've been searching for a urologist for us to go to…you know, a specialist, just to make sure everything is on track for us to get pregnant," she said, her eyes practically begging for a positive reaction.

"Sure, sounds good," I agreed. "Probably a good idea, in light of my situation."

The Diagnosis

After tests were administered on both Sue and me, we discovered that I could never give Sue a baby—at least, not in the traditional way. The doctor explained that either the bullet or the surgeries had given me an instantaneous vasectomy.

"I'm sure your surgeon's only goal that night was to save your life," the urologist said, "not to worry about whether you'd ever be able to reproduce."

"So, what are our options?" Sue asked. "I mean, of course, there's always adoption, but is there anything else we can do?"

"There is one possibility," the doctor explained. "The University of Michigan is doing a procedure called GIFT, which stands for gamete intrafallopian transfer, that is proving successful for couples in your situation."

The doctor went on to explain the procedure in detail, but what I understood was this—Sue's best eggs and my sperm would be placed together in Sue's fallopian tubes so that fertilization could take place in her body, as if conception had happened naturally. It all sounded like a lot of prodding, poking, extractions, injections, monitoring, and trouble; and, even with all of that work, they couldn't guarantee Sue would get pregnant.

So, we had our answer. We couldn't get pregnant the natural way, and that left us with very few options, all of which were long shots. A part of me wanted to say, "Hey, if we can't have kids, maybe it wasn't meant to be." But the bigger part of me wanted to give Sue her heart's desire, and that was a family. Still, I had my doubts.

"So, what do you think?" Sue asked on the ride home.

"I think it sounds interesting," I managed.

"What's wrong?" she asked.

"It's just that...seriously, how can I be a good dad without any legs? I mean, is it even possible to carry a baby in a wheelchair?"

"Of course," she insisted.

"And how will I throw a ball or push a swing or do the things a normal dad does?" I continued.

Without hesitation, she said, "You'll learn, and you'll be great."

And that was that. She wasn't worried, so I decided I would try to put my worries on the back burner and be the supportive husband she needed me to be. From what the doctor had described, the journey wasn't going to be an easy one....

FIVE

AND BABY MAKES THREE

During our first visit with the team at the University of Michigan, a GIFT specialist went over all the specifics with us, just as our referring doctor had done. Even as I heard it for a second time, I was completely overwhelmed with all of the details regarding the egg extractions, egg implantations, and so on.

"Cam, you'll have to give Sue shots every day," the doctor said, explaining that she'd need the shots to help her body prepare for pregnancy and to maintain that pregnancy once she had conceived.

"So, does this work for other couples?" Sue asked. "Couples like us?"

"Oh, yes," the doctor assured her. "We're having great success with this procedure. Of course, we can't guarantee anything. You might not get pregnant, or you might get pregnant with triplets."

"Triplets!" I interjected. "Really? Triplets are a possibility? Is that a strong possibility or just a minute chance?"

The doctor just smiled, and before he could answer, Sue asked him, "Do you have any idea how long it will take before I could get pregnant?"

"No way of really predicting that," he said. "But the good news is, you're here now, and we're going to get started right away."

With that, the doctor handed me a cup and asked me to give a sperm sample. I was embarrassed, but I was also more than willing to do whatever was necessary to make Sue happy.

And so "Operation Make a Baby" began.

On the two-and-a-half-hour drive home that night, Sue talked nonstop. I might've volunteered two or three words, but that was about all I could muster. Sue's first egg implantation was scheduled, and she was hopeful.

The next few years were filled with lots of ups and downs. It was an emotional roller coaster for Sue. Each day, when I gave her a shot in her backside, I would try to find a place that wasn't bruised from all the previous shots I'd administered. She was a trooper. As if it wasn't bad enough that the shots made her very hormonal, it seemed that everyone we knew started getting pregnant. Sue went to one baby shower after another, all the time wearing a fake smile and trying to hide the emotional battle raging within her. She wanted a baby more than anything, but the first few egg implantations hadn't taken, and there was no promise any would. We were traveling to the University of Michigan four to five times a year, in hopes the next procedure might be "the one" that would change our lives forever, all the while knowing we could end up childless at the end of the journey. On the plus side, our insurance covered all of the expenses associated with this experimental procedure. However, I could tell that the process was taking its toll on my wife.

"Hello?" Sue answered the phone in the kitchen of our new house. We had finally sold my trailer and purchased a three-bedroom, two-bath, 1500-square-foot ranch house. It was just what we needed to welcome a baby.

"Really?" Sue said, her voice cracking a bit. "Well, that's great news! Congratulations, Sis!"

When Sue hung up the phone, she was broken.

"My sister is pregnant," she shared, tears in her eyes. "And they weren't even trying for a baby."

I wanted to ask which sister, but I figured it really didn't matter at that moment. The reality was this: Sue's friends and family were all getting pregnant and having babies, and after several years of trying to make a baby, we were still childless. I didn't know how much more Sue could take.

I hadn't really prayed much since my time in the hospital following the shooting, but I wanted to pray. I wanted to pray for Sue. I wanted to ask God for help in this situation. I just wasn't sure how to reach out to Him. I mean, I knew He had spared my life. And I knew I had seen Him in a vision in those moments when I'd lingered between life and death. But I didn't really know God or understand anything about Him. Besides, I figured Sue was the pray-er of the family, and I was confident she had been praying about conceiving a baby, so I left it at that.

"It will happen for us," I consoled Sue, reaching across the counter to grab her hand. "I'm sure of it."

But I wasn't sure of it, and as the years passed, I was becoming less and less sure of it.

Good News

Once again, it was time for egg implanting at the University of Michigan, so we made the journey north. This time, the doctor implanted eight different eggs. The sheer number made me nervous, but, more than that, I could see that we were running out of options. It was sort of a now-or-never situation. After more than three years of trying, we were both tired—tired the drive to Michigan; tired of the poking and prodding; tired of getting our hopes up, only to be let down.

On a beautiful day in May 1993, I came home from work to find Sue acting very strange. As soon as my eyes met hers, I knew something was up.

"I went to the doctor today," she said.

"And?" I asked, hoping her smile meant what I thought it meant.

"I'm pregnant!" she gushed.

I hugged her and gave a grateful head nod toward heaven, thankful that we'd have a baby—or babies—of our own very soon. At that moment, we didn't know how many babies were on their way; we knew only that she was pregnant.

Later that month, we learned that only one of the eight eggs that had been implanted in Sue had been successful, so there was one miracle baby growing inside of her. From the moment Sue told me she was pregnant, the dynamics of our household changed entirely. Suddenly, every decision we made had to do with the baby. It seemed that we did not talk about anything else. We had every baby book imaginable, from *What to Expect When You're Expecting* to *The Best Baby Name Book in the Whole Wide World*.

With Sue due in December, I immediately went into "nesting" mode. I wanted to prepare the house for the baby. We had already decided which room would serve as the nursery; now we just had to decorate it. Since we didn't know if we were having a boy or a girl, we decided on a gender-neutral theme. While Sue picked out a border and bedding for the room, I began building a crib. I'd been a woodworker all of my life, but this project was different. It was more special and more precious than all of the other projects put together, and I wanted to treasure every moment I worked on that crib. So, I videotaped the entire process, thinking that, one day, I would show the footage to our child. From the time I got home from work until I went to bed, I worked diligently on the crib. I also made frequent runs to Subway to satisfy Sue's strange cravings for veggie subs. Though Sue wasn't feeling very good, physically, she was very happy. And, slowly but surely, I was coming around to accept the notion of being a father.

After years of heartbreak and disappointment, we were finally able to relax and just enjoy life. Lying in bed, I would often stare at Sue's growing belly and wonder about our unborn child. Would our baby be a boy or a girl? Would our baby look like me? Would our baby be healthy? Would our baby grow up OK with the fact that I had no legs? But, more than anything, I pictured myself being the father I'd never really had. I didn't want to screw up this chance to get it right. I fell asleep almost every night with my hand on Sue's belly, thankful for the miracle we'd been given.

It's Time

When Sue called me at work on December 13, 1993, her contractions were strong and coming pretty regularly. I hurried home and grabbed our hospital bag, which had been packed for weeks, and we headed for the hospital. While I completed paperwork at the hospital check-in, Sue was wheeled to a room, where she put on her gown and got ready for delivery. I thought Sue would give birth right away, but I was wrong. Hour after hour went by, and Sue's pain level increased tremendously. I felt helpless, because I couldn't do anything but feed her ice chips. With each contraction, she squeezed my hand so hard that I thought she would crush it; even so, the baby wasn't moving down like it was supposed to. After twenty-four hours of labor, the doctor said the words we didn't want to hear.

"We are going to do a C-section," he said calmly. "It's all very routine, but it's time to intervene. You're exhausted, and the baby is showing signs of distress."

As they prepped Sue for surgery, the nurse handed me a set of scrubs.

"Put these on," she instructed me. "We'll come and get both of you in a few."

Again, I wasn't exactly a praying man—never had been—but I figured if God had been able to bring me through my ordeal, then He could surely help Sue deliver our baby without any problems. As we headed for the operating room, I made my best attempt at a prayer, and I did feel a sense of peace come over me. Plus, I figured Sue was about as close to a saint as any present-day person I'd ever known, and I just knew that God was with her.

After what seemed like a lifetime of waiting, I heard the precious words, "It's a boy!" I cut the umbilical cord and held our son for the first time. He was perfect. He was beautiful. And he was all ours.

After Sue was stitched up, they brought our son into the hospital room. Sue kissed his tiny round head, as I sat proudly next to my family. We had a moment together before our extended family and friends came in to celebrate with us.

"He needs a name," Sue whispered, then looked at him. "Don't you, sweet boy?"

We had discussed girl names and boy names, but we'd never agreed on any as "the one." So, for that day, we just called him "our baby." That was meaning-ful enough. The following day, as I held him in my arms, I studied him and said, "Sue, I think he looks like a Braden. What do you think?"

"Braden...I like that," she said. "I like that a lot."

I don't know where that name came from, because it wasn't one we'd ever discussed before, but it was fitting. So, on December 15, 1993, Braden David Tribolet came into our lives.

As I fed him for the first time, he seemed very alert, so I told him something very important: "Braden, we wanted you so badly that we tried to make you for five long years."

"And you were worth all of the trouble we went through to have you," Sue added.

Sue and I smiled at each other and shared a moment of true bliss.

SIX

FROM RUSSIA WITH LOVE

Life with Baby Braden was hectic and happy. From 2 AM feedings to lots of dirty diapers to bath time, I tried to be a "hands-on" dad as much as possible. To be honest, I didn't know what I was doing half of the time, but Sue knew instinctively how to care for our baby, so she made up for my ignorance. As I watched Sue with our son, I marveled at her ways.

She really was born to be a mom, I thought.

She had not even healed from her C-section when she started talking about making another baby.

"It took us five years to make Braden," Sue said, while feeding him. "I think we'd better get started on a sibling for him, don't you?"

I didn't answer at first. I mean, I was just easing into this whole fatherhood thing, and the thought of beginning those trips to the University of Michigan again didn't seem that appealing.

"I guess," I mumbled. "Whatever you think."

Just a few months later, we were back at the university, showing off Baby Braden and trying for another. Doc performed the implant, and Sue and I headed home, hoping that God hadn't run out of miracles for us.

As Braden grew, I worried. *A son needs a dad who can throw a ball with him and build a snowman with him. I can't play sports anymore, and I can't even stand up in the snow. I hope I'm not a disappointment*, I thought.

I was fighting an internal battle, and Sue was fighting a physical one. Her body wasn't cooperating with the GIFT procedure, and we wondered if Braden might be an only child.

"The procedure was unsuccessful this time," the doctor said, looking directly at Sue. "I realize this is the first attempt for baby number two, but I have to be honest with you—I am not as optimistic this time around. It took five years to make your son, and you're older now, Sue."

I grabbed Sue's hand, knowing this news had to be killing her.

"My advice, guys?" the doctor said, looking at both of us. "Be thankful for your son, and if you really want another child, adopt."

We said our good-byes, thanking everyone at the university for the assistance and prayers, and then headed back to Fort Wayne. Sue was quiet for the first hour or so, and then she asked, "Well, what do you think?"

I knew I had to choose my words carefully and thoughtfully, so I took my time.

"I think the doctor was right," I finally said. "Honestly, Sue, I don't want to live through another five years of trips to the university, along with all of the emotional ups and downs. And I don't want to give you shots every day and watch you go through so much pain, all the while never knowing if we can even have another child.... I'm so happy that we have Braden. That's enough for me."

"But what if I want another child?" Sue said. "Are you open to the idea of adoption? I mean, I know we've talked about it before, but we never seriously considered it. How do you feel about it?"

"I'd definitely be open to it," I said, reminding Sue that my parents had adopted my sister when I was eight years old. "If you feel that's what we should do, then I think we should look into it."

That's all Sue needed to hear. By the time we pulled into our driveway, she had put the GIFT journey behind us and was already headed down the adoption path. And, this time, I didn't drag my feet; I went along willingly. I loved being

Braden's dad, and even though I still felt inadequate as a father, I wanted to be the best father possible. I figured that was enough.

Proving Ourselves

Sue's initial research on local adoption agencies was a bit disheartening. As soon as they found out that I was disabled—even though I had a steady job—we were no longer considered desirable parents. The more research Sue did, the madder I became. I just couldn't believe the discrimination we were facing. We were obviously capable of raising a child—we already had one! Meanwhile, other agencies thought we'd be good candidates to adopt a disabled child simply because I was disabled. That logic made no sense to me, either.

We made it past the initial interview, and the agencies sent field agents to our home to observe us. They toured our home and asked lots of questions, and they took many notes while watching us interact with Braden. I felt like I was living under a microscope, which totally played upon my internal fears of not being a good enough father.

What if we can't adopt a child because of me?

Thoughts like that tormented me at night. I'd lie awake, wondering if Sue would secretly blame me because she didn't have the life she wanted—a life with at least two children. I knew she was getting discouraged, and we were running out of options.

I let Sue do all of the adoption research and initial contacting, while I focused on being a good dad. Braden was growing up so fast. It was as if I'd blinked, and he was three years old. Sure, I couldn't do some of the same things that dads with legs could do, but I could still have fun with my son. He loved to roughhouse, so nightly wrestling matches had become one of our favorite activities. I would take off my prosthetic legs, making me about the same height as Braden, and the wrestling would commence. It was sort of like dwarf versus Braden, and he loved it. One night, after I had let him pin me, Braden celebrated his victory. Then he looked me straight in the eyes and asked, "Daddy, why don't you have any legs?"

I guess I always knew he would someday ask that question, and I wanted to be honest with him. But I didn't think that, at age three, he was ready to hear the full story of the shooting and my eventual amputation. So, without hesitation, I responded, "Well, I think God saw that I was running too fast in the other direction, and He needed to slow me down a bit."

And, just like that, Braden pounced on me for another round of wrestling. My answer was enough to satisfy him at that moment, but I knew that, someday, I'd have to share everything with him—just not until he was mature enough to handle it. And, honestly, I had spoken the truth. Though I hadn't really voiced it until that night, I truly believed that God had allowed the shooting to happen because, if it hadn't, I would have remained on that self-destructive path and probably would have killed myself, either through drugs or suicide. So, in a sense, dying had actually saved my life.

A Baby Sister

Finally, after years of searching and talking to many people about places to adopt, Sue found a promising agency: Hand In Hand International Adoptions, which had an office in Albion, Indiana. Braden was about to turn four, and we hoped that we could give him a baby brother or sister for his next birthday. He was old enough to understand what was going on, so we were very honest and open with him about our intentions.

"Hey, bud, would you like a baby brother or sister?" I asked Braden one day, while we were cuddled up on the couch together.

"Yes," he said, munching on goldfish crackers. "Maybe a sister."

Sue and I smiled at each other, knowing that Braden's wish might come true if everything went as planned with Hand In Hand.

The Hand In Hand people didn't mind that I was in a wheelchair. They didn't suggest that we adopt a handicapped child, even though I was handicapped. They simply wanted to see pictures of our home to make sure we had a suitable living environment, and they insisted that we take several mandatory parenting classes to prepare us for an international adoption. That was it! The interview process was much easier than the previous ones we'd undergone. I was finally feeling less like a failure and more like a father. They seemed happy for us to adopt a baby. It was the glimmer of hope we needed after the years of discouragement we'd endured.

Though we had our pick of adoptable children from around the world, we thought it best to adopt a European baby so she would look similar to us. After all, our child was already going to have to explain why her daddy didn't have any legs. We didn't want to make the transition any more difficult for our adopted child.

Just when we thought we had answered all of the agency's questions and finished all of the paperwork, the counselor who was working with us handed us the "God sheet"—at least, that's what I called it. Sue and I read through all of the various scenarios: "If your child is missing one eye, will you accept it?" "If your child is missing fingers, will you be OK with that?" On and on, the descriptive scenarios continued, and we just kept circling "Yes." Bottom line, we wanted a baby, and we kind of wanted a baby girl, since that was Braden's wish.

"Thank you very much," said Vicky Truelove, the adoption agency director, as she accepted our final paperwork and shook our hands. "We will be in touch."

Sue ran to the ladies' room, so I had a moment with Ms. Truelove by myself.

"I wanted to ask you something without Sue here," I told her.

"Of course," she said. "Go ahead."

"If you find a match for us, would you call me and let me know first?"

"Sure," she said, looking puzzled.

"I know that probably seems unorthodox, but since it's the wife who usually knows things first, I want to be the one to give Sue the good news," I explained. "OK?"

"You'll be the first one to know when we find a baby girl for you," she assured me.

As we left the adoption agency that day, I had a sense of peace. It just felt right, like everything was finally lining up.

About a month later, my phone rang at work.

"Mr. Tribolet?"

"Yes?" I answered.

"This is Vicky Truelove from Hand In Hand. We found a little girl for you who we think is a good fit. And I've already put a video of her in today's mail, so you should have it within the week."

"That's great news," I said. "Thanks so much for calling. I look forward to sharing the news with Sue."

I couldn't stop smiling as I dialed Sue's number at work.

"This is Sue," she said, in her professional tone.

"Baby, it's a girl!"

"What?" she screamed. "Cam?"

"I just heard from Vicky at Hand In Hand…they found us a daughter!"

I could literally feel her excitement through the phone.

About three days later, we received the package in the mail. By the time I got home from work, Sue had already opened it and was waiting to show me the VHS tape.

"I waited on you," she said, smiling. "I wanted to watch the video together—this could be our future baby!"

I sat next to Sue while Braden played with his favorite cars on the floor.

The letter that accompanied the video said, "She is in an orphanage in Russia…we think she might be a good fit for you."

As the video began playing, the sweetest little girl appeared on our TV screen. She immediately took my breath away.

"She's beautiful," Sue whispered. "I wish I could hold her right now."

According to the letter, the little girl was eight months old, but she looked much younger. Obviously, she was quite small for her age. We could only assume that she had been malnourished, which made us want to go immediately and take care of her. We felt an instant chemistry, an overwhelming empathy, and a deep love for her. I couldn't explain it; I just knew that this little girl was supposed to be our daughter.

"She's the one," I said. "She's our baby girl."

We didn't need to see any more videos or read any more letters—we wanted that child. She had already made an imprint on our hearts, and we had to have her. Of course, deciding we wanted her was the easy part. After we told our adoption counselor at Hand In Hand that she was the one, we had to hire a lawyer, complete more paperwork, and begin coordinating the adoption through the Russian embassy and the American embassy. Next, we were told to get our finances in order, which meant we needed to put our house up as collateral to generate the necessary money to take to Russia—between $12,000 and $30,000.

We knew, going into the adoption process, that it wouldn't be cheap, but we also knew that having a baby girl to call our own would be priceless.

The instructions from A to Z were very specific—get unmarked sequential $50 bills to take with us to Russia; meet a translator, who worked for the adoption agency as a liaison, at the airport; go with her to a family's home in Moscow, where we were to stay while the adoption details were worked out within the Russian courts; and plan to be away from home for about two weeks.

It had taken so long to get to that point, but when the time came to adopt, everything went so fast that it was overwhelming. Our stateside adoption counselor told us that our window of opportunity to get our baby girl was the following month, so Sue and I requested time off from work, asked Sue's mom to watch Braden, and prepared for the most important trip of our lives.

Meeting Our Baby

As we boarded our Moscow-bound flight in Fort Wayne, I couldn't help but think about the last time Sue and I had been on a plane together—when we'd traveled to the Bahamas for our honeymoon. So much had happened in the nine years since we'd said "I do." I never could have imagined that my life would be so blessed when I was lying on my back in that hospital bed ten years before. Back then, I was fighting for my own life. But this day, sitting next to my beautiful wife, the mother of my son, I was fighting for something else. I was fighting for my family. No matter what it took, I was willing to do it, if it meant we could bring our daughter home.

I slept off and on as we traveled from Fort Wayne to New York to Germany to Moscow. I couldn't wait to get off the airplane, and I couldn't wait to meet our baby girl. Just as our stateside adoption counselor had promised, a translator was waiting for us at the airport. She explained that our host family in Moscow was expecting us.

"When will we get to see our baby?" Sue asked her.

"Tomorrow," the translator said. "Get some rest tonight, and I'll be by in the morning with your driver."

Our hosts—a husband and wife—helped us carry our bags inside, giving us a welcome that was warm on several levels. I couldn't wait to get inside their home and out of the September heat. It was 101 degrees that day, but once we stepped inside their humble abode, we quickly realized that they didn't have any air-conditioning. I glanced over at Sue, who already had sweat beads forming on her forehead, and I knew what I had to do.

"Is there a shopping complex or a drug store nearby?" I asked our host family.

"Not far," the gentleman said, "I show you."

Thirty minutes later, I returned to find Sue sprawled out on the bed, trying to stay cool. I plugged in the fan, which at least circulated the warm air, and hoped we could get a good night's rest before tomorrow. I quickly undressed and removed my prosthetic legs, revealing the money stash inside each one.

"You stuck the cash inside your legs?" Sue asked.

"Yeah," I answered. "Pretty clever, huh?"

"I guess," Sue said, smiling. "I doubt anyone would suspect you had twelve thousand dollars stashed inside your legs."

"Exactly," I concurred, before kissing her good night.

The next day, we were up early, eager to meet our baby girl at the orphanage in Voronezh. Our driver and translator picked us up, and we headed toward the train station. The drive took us down a country road, with views of beautiful hillsides and gorgeous foliage. It wasn't at all how I had pictured Russia. I could tell Sue was anxious; I was, too.

When we arrived at the train station, we found that we had missed the train, so our only other option was to take a puddle jumper—a small airplane. When we finally arrived at the orphanage in Voronezh, we found that it was very traditional, very clean, and very much as I thought it would be. A woman greeted us, and the translator said something to her before she disappeared into another room.

"She went to get your baby," the translator told us.

Your baby.

I liked the way that sounded.

Moments later, we met our baby girl for the first time. The caregiver placed her in Sue's arms, and I captured the monumental event on film. She was skinny, and her hair was very thin. I knew those were signs of malnourishment, but I also knew the orphanage did the best it could for all of the children in its care.

When I inquired about her diet, I was informed that each baby was fed tea from a bottle, half of an egg yolk, bread soaked in milk, and a type of porridge on a daily basis.

"Would you like to feed her?" the caregiver asked through the translator.

I nodded, and the next thing I knew, I was feeding porridge to our sweet girl.

"She's a good eater," I said to Sue, who was stroking our baby's hair.

"I'm your mommy," Sue spoke softly to her, "and this is your daddy, and we love you very much."

We knew she didn't understand us at that moment, but we also knew we could spend a lifetime telling her how much we loved her.

Her Russian name was Yekaterina, which translates as Katherine in English. I really wanted to keep her Russian name, but Sue had her heart set on the name Julia, which seemed to suit our baby. Since we needed a name for her new birth certificate, we quickly decided on Julia Katherine Tribolet. After about an hour of cuddling the newest member of our family, Sue took her into another room to change her, while I took the last steps to make our adoption final. The translator explained that we needed to take a train into Voronezh, where we would meet with our lawyer and, eventually, the judge to finalize everything.

"We have to go catch a train, babe," I said to Sue, who was having a hard time leaving Julia.

Sue handed our baby to the caregiver, and I kissed Julia's cheek.

"Bye-bye, Julia," I said. "We'll be back to get you very soon."

As the caregiver took her into another room, Sue and I looked at each other and smiled. We would soon be a family of four.

The Final Step

We'd already consulted with our lawyer via our translator, so we knew what to expect when we appeared before the judge. It was interesting. In the United States, the adoption agencies wanted to hear from both Sue and me, but in Russia, they wanted to hear exclusively from me—the father.

"Why do you want a baby?" the judge asked me, through our translator.

"Because we already have one child at home that we love very much, and we desperately want another baby to love," I told her. "A baby girl would complete our family, and we are unable to have children any other way."

The judge continued asking questions in Russian, inquiring about my physical condition and my limitations. I told her all about the accident and how I had overcome so much with the help of God and Sue.

As the translator relayed my story, the judge nodded and gave me a sympathetic look. She then asked to see photographs of our house, which our lawyer provided. Since I didn't know any Russian, I was trying to follow their conversation, to no avail. I just hoped for the best and took a deep breath. After a few minutes, the judge made her decision and approved our adoption.

We were officially Julia's parents.

I hugged Sue and whispered, "Congratulations, Mommy."

And then, I thanked everyone around me. I think I even thanked a lawyer representing a different case…I was a little excited. We took the rest of the day to tour Voronezh and purchase souvenirs from Julia's homeland. I wanted to make sure that when she was old enough, we could tell her about her heritage and help her celebrate it with Russian dolls, trinkets, and so on. We also bought gifts for the orphanage, our host family, our translator, our driver, and anyone else who had helped us through the adoption process. We felt it was the least we could do, since we had been give so much.

Bringing Home Baby

When the caregiver at the orphanage handed Julia back to Sue, it just seemed like we had conceived her ourselves. We said our good-byes and thanked everyone at the orphanage. I was worried Sue was going to try to take a few more children with us. After all, she'd always wanted a large family. But she was content with Julia, and Julia was content in her arms.

We took care of some additional paperwork at the Russian Embassy in Moscow before it was time to head for the airport. Before we parted ways with our driver, I handed him my Gerber knife, because he had admired it earlier in the week. He was moved, and I was thankful I could give him something he would treasure.

As we stood in line at security, people stared at our baby and smiled, as if they were celebrating with us. I wanted to yell, "She's ours! She is officially ours!" Fortunately, Julia was a good traveler. She slept for much of the flight from Moscow to Germany. I held her and marveled at her sweet little face. She was very pale, almost translucent, and she was tiny; but she was beautiful. As we exited the plane in Germany, one of the flight attendants stopped us.

"Sir, would you and your family come with us, please?" he asked.

I nodded yes, hoping we weren't in trouble. I had already paid all of the money that had been hidden inside my hollow legs, so I hoped he wouldn't be asking for any.

I wonder what we've done? I thought.

"Enjoy our VIP room," he said, opening the door to reveal a very plush area.

I started to ask if he had us confused with someone else, but he interrupted me.

"We heard you just adopted that sweet little girl, and we thought you might want to relax, eat, drink, and spend your layover in here, before boarding the long flight to the US."

I was actually speechless. Luckily, Sue wasn't.

"Thank you so much," she said. "That means a lot to us."

I just stood there, grinning like an idiot, overwhelmed by his kindness.

Several other airline officials oohed and aahed over Baby Julia while Sue and I enjoyed the drinks and snacks. Before long, we were back on a plane headed for D.C., then Chicago, and then home. We knew our family would be waiting for us at the Fort Wayne airport, but we had no idea a TV crew would also be present. It turned out that one of Sue's sisters had shared our story with the local TV station, and they'd decided we were newsworthy. Our homecoming was captured on film, and even though we didn't look too good after twenty hours on an airplane, we couldn't have been happier. Sue held Julia like the proud mama she was, and I shared how we'd gone all the way to Russia to get our baby girl.

In all the excitement, I couldn't find Braden.

"Where's Braden?" I asked Sue.

"He is with Mom," she said, motioning for them to come over and meet Julia.

"Hey, buddy," I said, giving Braden a hug. "I missed you. I think you've gotten bigger since we left."

Sue knelt down to our five-year-old's level and said, "Braden, this is Julia—your very own sister."

Braden's eyes opened wide, and then he looked at me, as if to confirm what Mama had said. We were finally a family of four. It had taken ten years to build our family, but it had been worth the wait.

SEVEN

NEVER GIVE UP

The trip to Russia had been a whirlwind—exciting, exhausting, life-changing, and more. But as soon as we arrived back in Fort Wayne, it was business as usual. Back to work. Back to day care for the kiddos. Back to normal—as normal as our life could be, considering the circumstances.

With every day, Sue was bonding with Julia, and Braden was trying to get used to the idea of sharing Mommy and Daddy. After all, he'd had us all to himself for five years. It wasn't a difficult transition, but it wasn't picture-perfect, either, and I wanted to make sure that Braden knew he was still important to us. Therefore, I made sure to set aside a special "Daddy/son time" with him every night. Some evenings, we'd play video games. Other nights, we'd read books. And some nights, we'd wrestle.

Braden was five at the time and pretty big for his age.

"You're so strong," I encouraged him one night, as he jumped on my back to take me down.

But eventually, I overpowered him.

He immediately cried out, "I give up, Daddy. I give up!"

I rolled off of him, took his face in my hands, and said, "Don't ever say that, Braden. Don't ever give up! Do you hear me? Don't ever give up!"

"OK, Daddy," Braden said, obviously sensing the urgency in my voice. "I won't give up, I promise."

"OK, let's go again," I said, mussing his hair. "Best two out of three."

He thought we were just playing, but I realized later that it was much more than that. It had been a moment for me to impart wisdom to my son, and I had taken full advantage of it. I knew that if I could teach Braden that one life lesson—to never give up—it would carry him far. I knew that if I hadn't lived with a "never give up" attitude after being shot, I wouldn't have awakened from that coma in the hospital, I wouldn't have met and married Sue, and I wouldn't have had Braden and Julia.

As I thought back to that traumatic night, I was forced to revisit the visions I'd experienced while I was dead. I didn't want my mind to go there. I had blocked all of that out for a reason—because I wasn't ready to deal with any of it. Not yet. Though I had shared my visions with Sue, we'd never discussed what I had witnessed. And I hadn't spoken about them at all since leaving the hospital. I knew if I told other people that I had seen Jesus up close and personal, and that I had looked into the face of Satan, they would think I was insane. I mean, if I hadn't experienced it, I'd be questioning my sanity, too; but I knew it was real. I knew Jesus had spared me; I just wasn't sure why. I also knew I should probably be serving Him and making Him more of a priority in my life, especially since He had given me another chance. But I just wasn't ready to make that kind of commitment.

Enough for Now

"Cam, will you go to church with the kids and me tomorrow?" Sue asked as she climbed into bed next to me one night.

"You know I already have plans to go hunting," I replied, matter-of-factly. "Besides, I don't really get anything out of going to your church."

Sue was silent. She never nagged me, but I knew she was disappointed. I had basically lied to her and her family, letting them believe I was ready to become the best Catholic guy they'd ever met when I married Sue. In reality, I went to church on Easter and Christmas alone and had no intention of ever changing. That's just the way it was.

"Plus," I added, "hunting is very spiritual. It's just me and God and the quietness of nature. That's enough for now."

Hunting had become my escape from the day-to-day responsibilities of life, as well as my only real connection to God. It was more than a hobby to me, and it had been ever since I shot my first deer as a handicapped hunter, in 1988. The more I hunted, the more alive I felt. Out in the woods, sitting in a deer stand, waiting in the quietness of the morning, I didn't feel disabled; I felt like any other hunter. I sometimes wondered if other guys in my situation were also out there hunting, but it wasn't until 1995 that I found my answer.

I'll never forget that day. I was watching TV when *Buckmasters*, a show featuring disabled hunters, came on. I couldn't believe it! To see and hear the stories of the participants on TV really inspired me. At the end of the broadcast, a graphic popped up that said, "For more information, contact David Sullivan." I jotted down his phone number.

The very next day, I called David and shared an abbreviated version of my story, revealing that I had been disabled since 1986 and had started hunting again in the fall of 1988. I explained that I had been saving money so that I could go on a hunt outside of Indiana, someplace challenging and fun, and asked if he knew of any upcoming hunts I might get in on.

"I really want to try something outside my comfort zone," I continued. "But I don't want to go with someone who doesn't understand disabilities."

"I think I have a great contact for you," David told me. "His name is Ralph. He is a Canadian farmer with a lot of land, perfect for whitetail and mule deer hunts. He hosts hunts for disabled hunters several times a year. Give him a call and tell him that I told you to contact him."

"I will—thanks," I said, before hanging up.

I immediately called Ralph and really connected with him. After I'd told him a little bit about my story and explained why I wanted to hunt somewhere outside of Indiana, he invited me to go on a hunt at his place in early November. I could hardly wait. I called David back to thank him for the great contact, and I got more than a "You're welcome."

"So, you're for sure going?" David asked.

"Yes. It's all set."

"Great," David said, "because I'm going with you."

"You are?"

"Yes," he continued, "because I want to feature you in an upcoming issue of *Buckmasters Whitetail Magazine*. I want to interview you, let you share your story, and capture the details of the actual hunt."

I was overwhelmed, nervous, honored, and a little worried. *What if I don't get a deer?* I thought.

But I had said I wanted to do something outside of my comfort zone, and going on a deer hunt in Canada while being photographed and interviewed for a magazine was definitely out of my comfort zone.

It was a weeklong trip, and it was pretty intense. Canada was bitterly cold but absolutely beautiful. In between hunts, David and I talked about our families, our hobbies, our hopes, and so much more. As I shared all of the details of that fateful night in August 1986, I realized that it was the first time my story would be told in print. It was such a personal story, but I felt it was time to let others know what had happened. I wanted to offer hope to those who had suffered something as traumatic as I had. I wanted to tell them, "There is life after amputation, and it can be a wonderful life." And I wanted to tell them to never give up, which had become my daily mantra. The interviewing process was tedious but quite therapeutic for me. Yes, I had to relive everything as I shared my experiences in detail, but I knew my story had a purpose, and I knew it was time to tell it.

I had given David everything he needed for the story, except for an actual deer. We'd been hunting out of our vehicles, as well as from ground blinds, all week, and I hadn't shot a single deer. The deer seemed to be scarce, but I was determined to get one. Then it happened. I shot the biggest buck of the hunt. I was content, and David had a great lead for his story. All was right with the world.

On the trip back home, David and I relived my kill, and then David asked, "Ever been on a wild hog hunt?"

"Can't say that I have," I answered. "I hear it's very challenging, though."

"Yeah, it is," he confirmed. "I think you'd really like it. We've got a hog hunt coming up in the spring in Michigan…interested?"

"Absolutely," I said. "If I can get off work, I'm there."

Once I got back home, I couldn't stop thinking about hunting wild hogs in March. I was doing research on that type of bow hunt when I got a call from David concerning a January deer hunt in Alabama.

"Wanna come?" David asked.

"Of course!"

January arrived before I knew it, and I found myself in Alabama with a group of disabled hunters, all looking to shoot the biggest deer of the trip. The landowner made all of us move positions every day of the hunt, but on one particular day, I felt like I had found "the spot," and I didn't want to give it up. I asked the owner if I could return to that same deer stand the following morning. He agreed, and the camera crew, having overheard my conversation with the landowner, decided to film me there the next morning. They were amazed at how easily I shimmied up the tree to get into the deer stand, which stood about eight feet above the ground; however, it was just another day in the woods for me. I'd been climbing trees ever since Bobbie and I had built that makeshift ladder in 1988, so I didn't think anything of it. My thoughts were on the big buck that I knew was out there. I'd felt his presence the day before and knew it was only a matter of time before I found him. Then, after about two hours, that majestic buck came into view. I pointed my customized rifle at him and dropped him. It had been another successful Buckmasters hunt for me.

I felt so empowered. So capable. So normal.

Wild Hog

When March rolled around, I headed to Michigan to hunt wild hogs with my bow—a brand-new experience for me. Much to my surprise, I killed one—a huge one! It was my very first hog, and it was thrilling. It weighed 280 pounds— the biggest hog of the trip. Though I was making friends with the other disabled hunters and enjoying their companionship, bagging the biggest buck and now the biggest hog didn't make me the most popular guy.

"Very impressive," David said, checking out my kill.

"Thanks," I said. "I appreciate you letting me tag along on this one."

"I like you," David said, "and I think you'd make a great hunt coordinator for Buckmasters. You're good with people. You're very organized. And you're a good hunter."

"I don't know what to say."

"Say yes," he insisted. "I'm just too busy to do this alone anymore. All you'd have to do is research the hunts, schedule them, and act as the Buckmasters hunt coordinator in every capacity. And, of course, in return, you'd get to hunt for free."

Hunting in prime locations that cater to disabled hunters for free? I thought. *How can I say no?*

I called Sue that night to tell her about the Buckmasters opportunity, and she was tentatively happy for me.

"I sense some hesitation in your voice," I told her. "Do you not want me to take it?"

"No, I think you should definitely jump at this chance," she responded, "as long as it won't take you away from family too much. Promise me?"

"I promise," I said, assuring her that I'd use one of my vacation weeks for the hunts and the other week for family trips. Other than that, it would just be long weekend hunts a few times a year. Knowing how important hunting was to me, Sue agreed that this would be a wonderful opportunity and encouraged me to accept it.

So, I officially became a Buckmasters hunt coordinator in March 1996.

Little did I know that Buckmasters would play a vital role in bringing me back to God and helping me fulfill my destiny.

EIGHT

THE HUNT

I t's funny how you can fight so hard for something and then, once you have it, coast a bit and simply relax into the routine of life. That's exactly what had happened to me. I had fought with every fiber of my being to survive, and I did. I had fought so hard to walk again, and I did. I had battled to win Sue's heart and marry her, and I did. I had fought for an education and earned my first college degree. I had fought even harder for children, and we'd had Braden and chosen Julia. Sure, there had been ups and downs and twists and turns along the way. But, looking back over the road we had traveled, I could honestly say I would have done it all over again without changing one thing. The potholes, the detours, the rest stops—all of them had been important parts of the journey. They all had brought me to a place of routine happiness, where day-to-day life included a loving wife, two great kids, a job I liked, and a volunteer hunting coordinator position I adored. Life was good—as good as I thought I deserved—and I had no idea it could get any better. Of course, before better comes, it sometimes gets worse. What's that old expression—"It's always darkest before the dawn"? Well, it was about to get a bit darker....

Another Bump in the Road

"I freezin', Daddy," three-year-old Julia said, quivering, as I dried off her little body.

Bath time had always been my thing. Sue did most of the hands-on stuff, but I was the "bath man." Both kids always liked it when I gave them baths and made up silly stories about their bath toys. And, of course, it was tradition to sing funny bath-time songs and make crazy shampoo hairstyles.

As I was putting Julia to bed that night, I said what I always did whenever I had a chance to be alone with her and wanted to make her feel special.

"You know, sweetie, of all the babies in the entire world, we chose you to be our daughter."

She giggled. "How come?"

"Because you were the most beautiful, most special baby girl we had ever seen, and Mommy and I knew from the very first moment we saw you that you were supposed to our baby."

I kissed her on the forehead, and she grabbed my neck for a good-night hug. She had stolen my heart; there wasn't anything I wouldn't do for her.

"Daddy?" she called as I was leaving her room.

"Yes, sweetie?"

"When you take me to preschool tomorrow, will you give blood?"

"We'll see," I answered, remembering that the blood drive at her school would be going on all week. "Good night, honey."

The next morning was just like any other Monday morning—crazy, hectic, and exhausting. I rushed into Julia's preschool and gave her a quick good-bye hug. As I was getting ready to leave, Julia said, "Daddy, aren't you going to give blood?"

"Yeah, Daddy, aren't you going to give blood?" the woman running the blood drive teased.

"If you're giving away sugar cookies, I might consider it," I joked back, not really intending to give blood. I'd already had my share of needles for a lifetime.

"We are all out of cookies," she said, "but I'll have some for you tomorrow."

The next morning, I was greeted at the door of Julia's preschool with an entire bag of sugar cookies.

How can I refuse to give blood now? I thought. So, I rolled up my sleeve and did my good deed for the day, much to Julia's delight. Along with my cookies, they gave me an "I gave blood today" sticker, which Julia quickly claimed as her own, attaching it to her pink dress. Everybody was happy...until three weeks later.

Opening the mail that day, I noticed a letter from the American Red Cross. I figured it was a thank-you card, acknowledging my blood donation earlier in the month, so I opened it without much thought. But it wasn't a thank-you letter. It was a letter informing me that my blood had been deemed contaminated.

"Our tests confirm that you have hepatitis C and should seek medical treatment at your earliest convenience."

I must've read over that sentence ten times before handing the letter to Sue.

"Well, that's not good," Sue said, handing back the letter. "We need to call your doctor right away."

Apparently, when I had received those thirty-six pints of blood after the shooting in 1986, one of them had given me more than the gift of life—it had also given me hepatitis C.

Through additional tests, my doctor confirmed that I did, in fact, have hepatitis C, but it had been caught before the disease could destroy my liver. Still, the recommended course of treatment was not going to be fun. The doctor prescribed a year of interferon treatment, which is similar to chemotherapy. The treatment has a good chance of killing hepatitis C, but it makes you feel like death. Every day for a year, I had to give myself a shot of interferon in my stomach. I had a black-and-blue belly, felt sick all the time, and had no energy.

That year, I must have caught every germ going around, and with two children in the house, there were a lot of germs to be shared. Feeling ill much of the time, I lost twenty pounds, dropping down to my junior high wrestling weight of 167. I didn't feel good. I didn't look good. And I had no choice but to stick with the treatment for the entire 365 days.

One day, as I tried to find a place on my stomach that wasn't already bruised in order to give myself a shot, I thought, *Seriously, haven't I gone through enough in my life?*

But feeling sorry for myself had never been something I allowed myself to do for very long. I had my moments, but I snapped out of them pretty quickly. Instead of dwelling on the negative, I tried to be grateful that the hepatitis C had been found before it destroyed my body. If Julia hadn't insisted that I give blood at her preschool that day, I may never have discovered the hepatitis C until it was too late for treatment. So, I tried to look at it as a blessing in disguise. I seemed to have a lot of those in my life.

Divine Appointments

I had made it through the year of interferon treatments, and I was regaining my strength day by day. The treatment, no matter how awful it made me feel, never kept me from hunting. And, now that I was back to my normal self, I was really looking forward to the Buckmasters antelope hunt in New Mexico.

That particular hunt was especially sweet for our group of disabled hunters. Almost everyone got an antelope, and the camaraderie we shared was amazing. Sometimes, a group just clicks, and it did on this trip. It was our last morning, and I had just enough time to grab breakfast before heading to Albuquerque to catch my flight home. As I sat down with my bacon and eggs, I noticed a father and son sitting at the same table. I smiled at them, and the father struck up a conversation with me.

"So, what's with the film crew?" he asked.

"I am with Buckmasters…maybe you've seen the TV show? Anyway, we do hunts for disabled guys and kids. It's a great program."

"That's awesome," he said. "You know, I might want to get involved with something like that. I have about three thousand acres in Kansas that's pretty good for hunting. Would you guys ever want to host a hunt at my place?"

"We might," I said.

We chatted a bit more about Buckmasters, my involvement with the organization, and his land, and then we exchanged contact information before I headed to the airport. His name was Doug Eden.

It had been a good trip in every way.

After several phone conversations with Doug, I decided to pay him a visit in April 2004 to see if his acreage in Kansas would be suitable to host a future Buckmasters hunt. We spent a few days together and agreed that we'd do a deer hunt on his land in December of that year. He'd been a gracious host, and I was really looking forward to the hunt on his property.

Like always, I planned the Buckmasters hunt to the best of my ability. Even though it was a voluntary position, I took pride in what I did and loved every minute of it. On this particular hunt, we were accompanied by six disabled hunters. Doug's land was very good to us—each one of us got a nice buck. Doug and I not only enjoyed hunting together but also getting to know each other better. We discovered that we had a lot of things in common, and we were confident that our wives would be great friends if they had the opportunity to meet.

On the last day of the hunt, a Saturday, I was tired. I planned to go to bed early that night so that I would have plenty of energy to hit the road the following morning and drive the eleven hours home. Just as I was about to turn in, Doug stopped me.

"Hey, do you wanna join us for church tomorrow?" he asked.

"We'd love to have you," his wife chimed in.

Oh, man, I thought. *I don't want to go to church in the morning I have a long drive ahead of me, and I don't even go to church with Sue. What makes them think I'd want to go with them?*

But I felt sort of obligated to attend. After all, Doug had offered his land to us for the hunt. It was the least I could do, even though I didn't want to go at all.

"Sure," I answered. My stomach felt queasy at the thought of it. "What time do I need to be ready?"

"Starts at ten," Doug said. "See you in the morning."

As I sunk my face into my pillow that night, I could've kicked myself for not making up a good excuse as to why I couldn't go to church with them. He'd caught me off guard. Now, I had to go and just get through it.

The next morning, I followed the Edens in my truck, since I planned to leave for the airport right after church. As I pulled up to the parking lot, I had to smile. The view looked like a scene out of a Hallmark movie. There stood this cute little white church with a steeple on top.

Sue would think this is charming, I thought.

When we walked into church, each person greeted me, hugged me, and made me feel welcome. It was a far cry from the formality of most churches I'd experienced, and I kind of liked it.

"We're kind of into that 'hug and howdy' stuff," Doug joked.

"I can see that," I responded.

Inside the sanctuary, there were kids playing behind the wooden pews, which provided seating for about a hundred people. It was a small church, but what they lacked in numbers, they made up for in friendliness.

After a couple of worship songs, the pastor got up to speak and surprised me by welcoming me from the pulpit. All eyes turned to me. I was embarrassed, but I smiled just the same. As the service continued, I felt the most amazing peace come over me. I actually felt warm all over, like somebody had turned up the heat. I didn't follow everything the pastor said, but I liked it. I liked this church. For the first time in my life, I actually enjoyed being in church. I had no idea why, but I had a very good feeling just being there, surrounded by the friendliest folks I'd ever met. After church, they had a potluck dinner, which included fried chicken, mashed potatoes, green bean casserole, corn bread, and some of the best desserts known to man. I ate to my fill before I told Doug I needed to get on the road. As I headed for the door, I was bombarded by hugs and good-byes.

"Thanks for everything, Doug," I said as I walked to my truck.

"You're welcome," he said. "Don't be a stranger."

"I won't."

For the next eleven hours, I thought about that little white church, its wonderful people, and the way I'd felt from the time I'd entered its doors until I'd left. Something had changed on the inside of me. I could feel it. I couldn't explain it, but I knew something was different. I couldn't wait to tell Sue about Doug's church.

Now, if Sue could find a church like that in Fort Wayne, I thought, *I'd go every Sunday.*

God must've known what I was thinking, because He was just about to see if I meant it.

NINE

FINDING THE WAY

I t was funny—while I was deer hunting in Kansas, Sue had been church hunting in Fort Wayne, and we'd both been successful.

"Good to have you home," Sue greeted me at the door.

"Good to be home," I said, giving her a kiss.

"So, I know I probably shouldn't bombard you when you first walk in the door, but the kids are in bed, and there's so much I want to tell you," Sue said, hardly taking a breath.

"That's fine," I replied. "I have stuff to tell you, too. You first."

"So, you know I've been church shopping lately, right?" she asked, and then continued talking before I could answer. "Well, today I found a church that I really like. It was warm and inviting, and the pastor was funny and engaging. And they even had a great kids' program for Braden and Julia. So, will you go with us next Sunday? I already checked your calendar, and there are no hunts booked...."

I hadn't seen Sue this excited about anything in a while. I loved it when she got worked up over something, because she would talk a mile a minute and kick her normal level of bubbliness up several notches. How could anyone say no to her?

"Of course," I answered, smiling at her cuteness.

"Really?" she asked, obviously surprised that I'd given in so easily.

"Yeah, really," I said. "I know it seems odd, but the church you're describing sounds a lot like the church I went to this morning."

She gasped. "You went to church today?"

"Uh-huh," I answered. "Don't be so shocked. Doug, the guy who hosted the hunt, asked me to go to church with his family this morning, and I thought it would be rude to say no, so I went. And, Sue, it was exactly what you said. The people were friendly and warm. The pastor was funny and engaging. I actually enjoyed it."

Sue just sat there, smiling. Speechless. I don't know if she was in total shock that I had actually gone to church or just really happy that I'd agreed to go again. Either way, I was glad my news had put a great big smile on her face.

After missing work for the Kansas hunt, I was playing catch-up. It was a busy week, which made the days go by quickly. The following Sunday, we woke up early. Sue fixed Julia's hair while I ate breakfast with Braden in the kitchen.

"What did you think of church last Sunday?" I asked Braden, between bites of cereal.

"It was pretty cool," he said. "I liked it better than our other church."

That was quite a positive endorsement from a quiet eleven-year-old. Now it was my turn to form an opinion.

Just for Me

As we took our seats in the pew at Grabill Missionary Church, I thought it was a nice place. It was bigger than Doug's church, but the people were just as friendly. After the singing portion of the service, Pastor Bill Lepley greeted the congregation and began his message. As he spoke, I felt sure Sue must have told him all about me and my history, because everything he was saying seemed like it was just for me.

"Did you talk to this pastor about me?" I whispered to Sue.

"No," she whispered back, "I wouldn't do that without your permission."

I knew Sue was telling the truth, yet I wondered how this pastor knew exactly what to say to draw me in. I'd always thought of God as some big guy in the sky who had a heavenly club that He would use to whop you upside the head whenever you did something wrong. But Pastor Bill spoke of a loving heavenly Father who wanted a relationship with me. I'd never had much of a relationship with my earthly father, so I had a hard time comprehending a father's love—especially unconditional love.

"No matter what you've done or how far you've strayed, God still loves you," Pastor Bill proclaimed.

How could He still love me? I thought. *I have done so many bad things in my life.*

My mind drifted back to my growing-up years. I had basically been addicted to drugs and alcohol from age fourteen to twenty-three, and I had done unspeakable things to finance my drug habit. I had prostituted myself at a bar one night because the woman promised to pay me in cocaine. I had stolen money from my own parents and blamed it on my friends, just so I could buy more speed. I had run a successful drug ring in high school, cutting drugs and selling them, as well as luring others into addiction. And I had been kicked out high school for having a .25-caliber gun in my pocket and a bowie knife strapped to my leg. So many bad things....

When Pastor Bill asked us all to bow our heads and pray together, I prayed for the first time in many years. I wasn't sure exactly what to pray, so I was glad he led us through a prayer that I could just repeat.

I wasn't sure what had happened during that service, but I knew I felt better.

After the service, we went out for lunch, and I told Sue that I liked the new church and would be willing to go back again. But it wasn't until that night in bed that I was really able to open up to her about what I had experienced that morning.

"So, you really liked church today?" Sue asked, cuddling next to me in bed.

"I did," I affirmed. "I liked a lot of what the pastor had to say. I even prayed the prayer with him at the end of service."

"You did?" Sue asked, turning over to look at me.

"Yeah, and I don't know what happened, but I feel better...like, a lot better."

"That's what happens when you give God control of your life," Sue confirmed. "He makes everything better."

It was the end of 2004, and I knew in my heart that 2005 was going to be a wonderful New Year. After all, I had a new beginning.

All-in

Someone once pointed out to me that I'm an all-or-nothing kind of guy, meaning that when I go after something, I am all-in. If I'm not going to give it 150 percent, then I just won't do it. That kind of mentality can be both a blessing and a curse. At times, it can come across as stubborn and unfeeling, but when all of that energy and passion are geared in the right direction, it can be very powerful.

When I was keeping God at an arm's length and running the wrong direction all of those years, I was going all-out. I had no interest in following God or making a commitment to Him. But once I experienced God in that little white church in Kansas, and then again at Grabill Missionary Church the following Sunday, I was all-in. I couldn't get enough of Him. So, when a guy from Grabill Missionary Church asked me to join several other men from our church at a Promise Keepers convention in town, I agreed to go. The theme of the conference that year was "The Awakening," which I thought was quite fitting, since I had experienced a real spiritual awakening just four months prior. I didn't know much about Promise Keepers, but I did know they stood for godly men and healthy marriages, so I thought it would be good for me.

I was right.

As I listened to these successful men share their stories of tragedy and eventual triumph, I was moved. The message came across loud and clear: "Nothing is too big for God!" As I looked around, there were men of all ages, races, and socioeconomic backgrounds, and they were all praising God. It was powerful.

"If these stories have inspired you, and you are going through struggles today, too, remember that nothing is too big for God," the speaker said. "He had the solution before you ever had a problem. Just put your faith in Him right now. Come on down if you want prayer."

His words pierced my heart, and I immediately released the brakes on my wheelchair and rolled down to the front. I did want prayer. In fact, I wanted everything God had for me. I was all-in.

Several men laid hands on me and prayed that God would use me to make a difference in the world and help me become the man that He had called me to be. As they did, tears streamed down my face. I wanted both of those things. I just hadn't realized it until that very moment.

That entire summer was very special. Since I had changed on the inside, I wanted to make it official and share my transformation with the world by getting baptized. So, in August 2005, Pastor Bill arranged to baptize me in a pond in northern Indiana. I was so excited. I wanted everybody important in my life to be there for the big day. I especially wanted Doug Eden to come. After all, he was the one who had started me on the journey back to God with his simple church invitation the previous year.

I called to invite him. "So, will you come?" I asked, awaiting Doug's response on the other end of the line.

"Of course, I'll be there," he said. "Wouldn't miss it."

I had hoped my parents would feel the same way, but both Dad and Mom declined my invitation. I guess I wasn't surprised, since they really hadn't had much to do with me or my family since the wedding, but I was still disappointed. I wanted them to know God the way that I finally knew Him, but I couldn't force them to come.

When the day of the baptism finally arrived, I was nervous.

"You're going to do great," Sue encouraged me. "God's given you an awesome story to share, so just share it."

She was right.

I said a silent prayer, asking for God's divine direction as I spoke, and then I just opened my mouth. I don't know exactly what I said, but when I looked around at my family and friends, everyone was crying.

Well, it was either a really good testimony or a really bad one, I thought. I hoped it was the former.

Then Pastor Bill baptized me in that little pond, and I came up out of the water feeling better than I'd ever felt before. It was just like the words of that old hymn we sometimes sang in church, "Joy unspeakable and full of glory." That's how I felt.

A New Way

Having a relationship with God made everything sweeter. I'd heard Christians say that very thing, but I'd always thought that it was just something they said to sound spiritual. I had to experience it for myself to realize the truth of that statement. As I followed God, He opened doors and lined up divine appointments for me when I least expected them. For example, I first met my good friend Roger Devenport in 2000. I was on a Buckmasters hunt in Utah, scheduling a future mule deer hunt for a group of disabled men, when we first connected. He overheard me talking about the upcoming hunt, and he stopped me later at the evening campfire.

"You know, I have a hunting ranch in northern Wisconsin," he said. "I'd be interested in hosting a hunt for disabled children."

"That's great," I responded, then inquired about his land and asked how much he would charge us to use his ranch.

We settled on a very reasonable price that would cover the costs of lodging and meals, and I set out to raise the needed funds. However, when we actually arrived at his thousand-acre hunting preserve months later, he wouldn't accept the money. He'd had a change of heart and just wanted to be a blessing. That was the beginning of a very important relationship in my life. Over the years, we hosted dozens of disabled hunts on Roger's land, and our friendship grew stronger every year.

In early 2007, Roger retired and ended up selling his hunting ranch, but we kept in touch. Later that year, we were sitting in a restaurant in Buffalo County, Wisconsin, when he said, "I miss this—I miss being a part of these hunts."

I sensed he had more to say, so I just listened.

"You know, after reading Rick Warren's *Purpose Driven Life*, I know my purpose," he continued. "My purpose is to help disabled hunters and terminally ill children who want to hunt. What do you think about helping me start a hunting organization that caters to those two groups?"

"I would love it," I said. "And we could start a magazine or something to showcase the hunts and bring attention to the disabled hunters, the kids, and the sport."

"Nah," Roger replied. "I say go big or go home. Let's do a TV show."

"I'm in," I said.

And just like that, The Way Outfitters Outdoor Adventures was born. We determined it would be a faith-based charitable organization providing outdoor adventures for disabled or terminally ill children, as well as disabled veterans. And we came up with lots of ideas, such as giving each hunter a camouflage Bible to commemorate the hunt. We knew our biggest challenge would be funding the hunts, but we weren't worried, because God had always provided in the past, and we were both sure that this wasn't just a good idea—it was a God idea.

As the director, Roger has devoted so much time and energy to The Way Outfitters. His dedication to the organization only goes to show how far he is willing to go for his faith and to fulfill his purpose—extending hope to terminally ill and disabled children and veterans.

Of course, in order find enough time and energy to volunteer as activity director for The Way Outfitters, and also to support *The Way Outfitters Adventures*—the TV show we eventually started—I had to walk away from Buckmasters after serving with them for ten years. But I knew it was the fulfillment of the prayer the men had prayed over me at the Promise Keepers meeting in the summer of 2005, that God would use me to make a difference in the world and help me become the man He had called me to be. With the birthing of The Way Outfitters, I felt I was closer to fulfilling both of those charges.

Mt. Whitney Climb
(July 2013)

Sue and I at the trailhead of the Mountaineers Route on Mount Whitney. This is where hiking turned into rock climbing.

As you can see, the rocks were more like boulders.

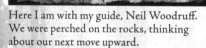

Here I am with my guide, Neil Woodruff. We were perched on the rocks, thinking about our next move upward.

Fulfilling a lifelong dream of mine to ascend and rappel. From this angle, you can see the mountain-climbing legs from SRT Prosthetics & Orthotics.

Posing with my first turkey and my good
hunting buddies Curt Cardman (left) and
Bobbie Poynter (right) in April 1996 in
Pennsylvania.

Braden with his springbok on our African
safari in April 2009.

Elk hunting in Capitan, New Mexico, while
on a Buckmasters hunting trip for the
disabled. If it wasn't for volunteers like Joe
Hesseling (pictured here), I would not have
had this opportunity.

Hunting trip in Hondo, Texas, while filming an
episode of *The Way Outfitters Outdoor Adventures*.

Sports

Monoskiing at the top of Mary Jane Mountain in Winter Park Resort, Colorado, at about 12,000 feet. What a view!

On a memorable trout fishing trip with my father-in-law on the Colorado River near the Grand Canyon.

Parasailing in Ixtapa, Mexico! The best part of the flight was seeing these guys' faces as they were getting ready to catch me. My life was literally in their hands.

Family

A recent family photo taken at Grabill Missionary Church in November 2013. My oh my, how the family has grown.

On a pond in Girard, Pennsylvania, trying to catch some crappie for dinner. Yes, the kids caught more than I did.

Our very first time meeting our precious, beautiful baby girl, Julia, in Voronezh, Russia. An unforgettable day.

A beautiful father-and-son moment I'll never forget.

TEN

A TRIP TO REMEMBER

I had heard of the Safari Club International's Pathfinder Award, given each year to two hunters who have overcome a physical challenge with a "never give up" attitude, serving as an example for others facing similar challenges. However, I never thought I would be nominated for such a prestigious honor. But Sue thought I should be considered, so she wrote a very flattering letter about me and submitted it in 2008. In her letter, Sue talked about the shooting and my injuries, my eight-month hospital stay, my multiple surgeries and double amputations, and my will to get better, despite the odds. She highlighted the work I had done with Buckmasters and The Way Outfitters, as well as my determination to never let my disability define me. Her thoughtful letter was reward enough for me, and I was touched that she'd taken the time to write such a marvelous tribute. Sue had always been my hero; it was nice to learn that I was also hers.

Because so many deserving people are nominated each year, I was completely overwhelmed when I discovered that not only had I won, but I had also been named Pathfinder One, which meant I got to choose between two hunting trips— Africa or Argentina. It was a no-brainer for me, because I had always dreamed of going on an African safari but could never afford it. The award included the cost of the hunt for me and one companion, all of our food and lodging in an upscale resort, a personal hunting guide, and taxidermy services, including shipping and handling expenses.

After I calmed down from the initial shock of winning, I realized this opportunity had created a small problem—deciding whom to take with me. I could take only one person, but there were three people I really wanted to accompany me—Sue, Braden, and Bobbie. It would seem only fair that I take Sue, because she had nominated me, thereby making the trip possible; plus, she is my very best friend. However, she doesn't hunt, and I knew she might get bored being by herself all day while I was on safari. On the other hand, Bobbie is the one I credit for really getting me back into hunting, and I knew he would be a great safari buddy. And then there was Braden, my fifteen-year-old son, who enjoyed hunting and just hanging out with his dad. I couldn't decide. Regardless of who I took, I knew it would be the trip of a lifetime.

Sitting on the couch, I discussed my dilemma with Sue. She had always been the voice of reason, and I respected her advice. Without hesitation, she said, "While I'd love to go with you, I think you're right—I might get bored spending two weeks in a place that caters to hunters. You can only do so much sightseeing, you know?"

"True," I agreed.

"And you and Bobbie would have a great time," she continued, "but I think he would understand if you took Braden. This could be a wonderful, once-in-a-lifetime trip for the two of you. Of course, we'd have to see if he could be excused from school for two weeks."

It was settled, then. I would ask Braden if he wanted to go.

Moments later, I called for Braden, who was doing homework in his room.

"Yeah, Dad?" he said. "What's up?"

"You know that award I won that includes an African safari?"

"Yeah."

"Well, would you like to go with me?"

"Yeah!" he said, his eyes full of excitement. "Are you really asking me?"

"Yes, I'm really asking you," I assured him. "I think it will be a really special time for us."

"That's awesome."

Minutes later, I heard Braden talking on the phone to one of his friends, sharing the details of his upcoming African safari. I had obviously made the right choice. He was just as excited as I was.

Even though Sue had given up her spot on the safari, she accompanied me to the Pathfinder Award ceremony in Reno in January 2009. That was much more of a "Sue trip," anyway. They put us up in a gorgeous suite with VIP tickets to all of the shows and more. It was fitting to have her by my side when I received the Pathfinder Award and gave my acceptance speech. After all, I wouldn't have been up on that podium if she hadn't written such an amazing nomination letter.

While at the Pathfinder event, we met with a travel agent who booked mine and Braden's trip and took care of all of our hunting permits and other paperwork. I even got to meet our trip guide. It had been almost a year since I'd been named the recipient of the award, but with the safari almost upon us, I was just as excited as the moment I'd first heard about the African safari—a trip that would easily cost between $40,000 and $50,000. I was so honored, humbled, and grateful.

As I said good-bye to our guide, I took a moment to thank God. *You are so good to me, God. Even when I fall short, You still love me. Thank You, God, for this amazing opportunity.*

Big Game, Big Love

Our trip plans had been finalized, and I had been given permission for time off from work, but I hadn't yet cleared it with Braden's high school. I was a bit nervous to ask that he be excused for two whole weeks; however, he was a very good student, so I hoped it would be doable.

"Looking at Braden's grades thus far in the semester," the principal said to me, peering over his glasses, "I'd say he could be gone two months and he'd still make straight A's. And I'm sure this African safari will be very educational itself. Have a safe trip."

"Thank you so much," I said, shaking his hand.

So, that was it. We were off. We said good-bye to Sue and Julia and boarded our long flight to London. The guide shared with us that we'd be staying at a hotel at Heathrow Airport for one night to rest before embarking on one of the greatest adventures of our lifetime. We could hardly wait.

On the flight from London to Hosea Kutako International Airport in Windhoek, Namibia, I wondered about how Braden would do without any TV, radio, or video games for two whole weeks. But he had always been mature for his age, so I was confident he would do all right. And I secretly wondered if I'd be able to keep up my stamina on such physically demanding hunts each day. I was stronger than I had ever been, able to do more than I thought I could, but I was still the guy with prosthetic legs. That was just a fact.

Braden and I were overwhelmed by the majesty of the landscape as we tried to take it all in during the two-hour drive to Mount Etjo, where our resort was located.

"Dad, look!" Braden said, pointing to a giraffe running alongside our vehicle.

In fact, we saw so many giraffes that we nicknamed the area "Giraffic Park." It became our little inside joke during the safari. We also saw warthogs and other animals running wild. The sights took my breath away. It was like something out of a movie, yet we were seeing it firsthand.

The resort was fit for a king. We arrived just in time to watch one of the most beautiful sunsets I'd ever seen, viewed through the floor-to-ceiling windows in the two-story loft area. The other hunters had also arrived. They included a guy from Columbus, Indiana; a husband and wife from the East Coast; and three professional guides. I was the only disabled hunter, but I was pretty sure I was also the most experienced hunter. Then, just as our stomachs started to growl, the camp manager described our upcoming dinner in detail, noting that our meals for the duration of our stay would be prepared by an award-winning French chef.

"Sweet," Braden said.

It was no wonder he was an award-winning chef, because the food was delicious. Course after course of beautiful, rich, exotic dishes were placed before us.

"I could get used to this," I said to Braden, taking another bite of my steak.

We retreated to our room, prepared our guns for the next day's hunt, and went to bed, dreaming of hunting wild game. Our trip was off to an amazing start.

The next morning, we had a breakfast fit for kings. Looking at all the pastries and waffles, I was sure I'd gain at least ten pounds before the trip was over. As good as the food tasted, I was almost too excited to eat.

"Are you two ready?" asked Rudy, our personal guide.

"Yes," I answered, downing one last sip of orange juice.

As we headed out to hunt, the sun was just coming up over the beautiful landscape. We rode in a strange kind of vehicle that was sort of like a dune buggy with a mobile tree stand on top of it. That's where Braden and our hunting dog rode. There was no windshield, so we were able to get up close and personal with the African landscape. The tall grasses brushed my face as we tore through the terrain. The sights, sounds, and smells were unlike any place I'd ever been, and our guide was great because he told us about everything—the foliage, the animals, the customs, and so on. I was so glad I was getting to experience this awesome place with my son.

The month of April is autumn in Namibia, and every day was sunny and 70 degrees—perfect. And talk about great hunting! Braden and I were able to hunt so many exotic animals. It was very challenging, and very different from sitting in a deer stand, waiting for a good shot. One day, I headed out on my crutches, stalking a zebra for two hours across the African plains, until I finally got my shot.

Day in and day out, we awoke before sunrise, ate a tremendous breakfast, and hunted to our hearts' content. We already had fourteen animals, so there was no pressure to get "the one that got away," because we hadn't let any of our targets escape. Knowing this, Rudy said something I'll never forget:

"Let's stop hunting for the day," he said. "I want to show you things. I want you to experience Africa for Africa."

Braden and I looked at each other and nodded in agreement. We put up our guns and went on a day of discovery with Rudy. After driving a bit, he stopped the vehicle and grabbed a plant. Then he broke it open, pulled it close to his face, and inhaled.

"Smell this," he instructed me, holding the plant close to my nose.

"That smells really good," I said, passing it on to Braden.

Rudy told us about many flowers and the healing properties of various plants. Then he drove us to the top of a big hill, probably a couple of thousand feet high, and stopped.

"Look at that," he said, with pride in his tone. "Have you ever seen anything so beautiful?"

It really was beautiful. Below us were green fields dotted with colorful flowers, and dozens of animals running through the tall grass, while others basked in the late-afternoon sunshine. I did shoot that day, but my weapon of choice was a digital camera, and I pointed it and shot many times during our day of discovery.

It was our last day of the trip, and I was so thankful Rudy had suggested abandoning our hunting plans and going on a different kind of adventure with him. The sun was just setting in all its fiery orange glory, and I snapped a picture at just the right moment. As I stood there with Rudy and Braden on the hilltop, I knew I'd never forget that moment as long as I lived. There was something very spiritual about Africa, about Rudy, about the entire experience, and it wasn't even over yet.

My Modern-Day Knight

By the time we made it back to the resort, we were late for dinner, but we didn't care. Our day had been perfect. Thankfully, there was still enough food for us, and we enjoyed our final dinner by the big fire pit, underneath the stars. Braden and I chatted about our favorite hunts and how we hated to leave such a wonderful place, but we agreed it was time to go home.

"Ready to call it a night?" I asked Braden as he was finishing his dessert.

"Yeah, I'm so full," he said. "Really gonna miss this food...wish that chef could come home with us."

"We better not tell your Mom that," I teased.

Braden thought we were just going back to our room to pack, but I had a surprise for him that I'd been planning for weeks. I had wanted to do something special for him ever since my Sunday school class at church had begun studying the book *Raising a Modern-Day Knight* by Robert Lewis. In his book, the author encourages parents to recognize important milestones in a son's life and commemorate them. This hunting trip was an important milestone. I watched a fifteen-year-old boy become a man right before my eyes, and I wanted him to know how proud I was of him and how much I loved him.

Braden had always loved my customized 7mm Magnum rifle because it shot so smoothly and precisely—high power but little to no recoil. Because my shoulders had needed to be replaced due to wear and tear from using crutches and canes for so many years, that gun was perfect for me, because I couldn't have a gun with regular recoil; it was just too painful. It was tailored with all of my needs in mind, and we had shot all fourteen animals that trip with my gun.

"Braden, come here a minute," I told him. "I want to talk to you."

He put down the clothes he was packing and sat down across from me.

"I just wanted to tell you how proud I am of you," I began. "We got up crazy early every morning, and you never whined one time. And whenever Rudy or I needed help, you were right there. Even though we asked a lot of you every day, you never complained at all. You may have started this trip as a boy, but you're ending it as a man, and I couldn't be prouder of the man you've become."

Braden just shook his head and smiled, very emotional and very touched.

"That's not all," I continued, grabbing my gun from the gun safe. "I think I have shot every animal I could ever shoot with this gun, and you know how much this gun means to me. But, starting today, I want you to start making memories with it."

I handed the gun to Braden, and he took it and looked at it like it was a prized treasure. And it was.

"Is it really mine?" he asked.

"Absolutely," I said.

The next morning, as we grabbed our luggage and headed out, I looked over at the gun case and said, "Braden, don't forget your gun."

He smiled at me in a way I'll never forget, grabbed his gun, and said, "Thanks, Dad."

I looked up to heaven and said the same thing.

ELEVEN

ENDINGS AND BEGINNINGS

C am, seriously, you need to get away," Sue said. "You're scaring me. You're stressed all the time. You're barely eating. You're not getting any sleep. You're just not yourself."

"I'd love to get away, but with Mom and Dad both in separate nursing homes—neither one doing very well—and the stuff going on at work, I just don't see how I could go hunting this weekend."

"Listen, you aren't the only child in town. Just call your brother and tell him that you need to get away for a few days and ask him to look in on your parents," Sue suggested. "You need to accept the fact that you can't be everything to everyone. You don't have to solve every crisis, and you certainly don't have to do it before Monday. And, as far as work goes, it's been crazy hectic there for months now, and we both know that it's totally out of your control."

That's one of the things I love most about Sue—the way she supports me no matter what. She is always on my side—my constant cheerleader, my confidante, my best friend, and always the voice of reason.

Taking her advice, I did call my brother Tracey to let him know I was heading out of town for a quick deer hunt in Texas but would check in on both Mom and Dad before leaving.

I stopped in to see Dad and told him I'd be gone a few days but that Tracey would be by. He gave me the typical grumble. He was still the unhappiest man I'd ever known.

On the drive across town to Mom's nursing home, I couldn't help but think how much easier it would be if Mom and Dad were in the same facility. That had been the original plan after Mom's last stroke, when the doctor had said she could no longer care for herself, but Dad wouldn't hear of it. They had divorced in their early seventies—mad, miserable, and lonely—and he wanted nothing to do with her.

"Mom," I said, upon entering her room. "How are you today?"

She hadn't been able to speak in several months, but I hoped she could understand me.

"The floor nurse said they are going to have movie night tonight," I added, "so that will be fun for you."

I tried desperately to make conversation, but when you're the only one talking, it's difficult.

"Listen, Mom. I have to go out of town for a few days, but Tracey is going to stop by and see you, OK?"

She just stared at me, this shell of a woman. The strokes had stolen almost everything from her, but I still thought she might be in there somewhere when I looked into her eyes. Every time I visited, I grew sadder—sad that she hadn't been a mom to me, sad that she hadn't tried to rectify the situation once I became an adult and had a family of my own, and sad that she didn't know my children at all. As pathetic as I knew it was, I think I visited her regularly in hopes of finally earning her approval. Since my older brother had pretty much divorced himself from the family, and my sister lived in Washington, D.C., and Tracey rarely visited because of his crazy schedule, I thought I might finally be the favorite.

"Bye, Mom," I said. "I'll see you real soon, OK?"

Just like I had done at Dad's nursing home, I chatted with Mom's doctor and made sure she wasn't in critical condition.

"I just don't want to go out of town if she's going downhill," I confided to the doctor.

"Understood, but listen—go ahead and go," he said. "She is stable. We'll call you if anything changes."

As I drove home to pack, I had an uneasy feeling about leaving that weekend, yet Sue was right—I did need some time away. Not only were my parents weighing heavily on me, but my work situation had become a nightmare. Since I was district manager, when corporate wasn't happy with our sales figures, it all fell on my shoulders. But it really wasn't my fault our sales were down—everybody's sales were down. In fact, another fire sprinkler installation company in town had closed its doors the week before. With the economy still in a downward spiral, sales of all kinds were hurting.

Once I landed in Texas, I felt better about everything. I was meeting with Roger, my friend and confidant at The Way Outfitters; another disabled hunter; and Sam Santa-Rita, our hunt sponsor from SRT Prosthetics & Orthotics of Fort Wayne, Indiana. It was already early evening, so after Roger and I settled in at our lodging in Kerrville, we shared some good food and decided to call it a night, since we both had to be up extra early to manage the logistics of the hunt.

Just before turning in, I set the alarm on my phone, as I always did, and then I drifted off to sleep. I don't know if it was the stress of everything or just fat fingers, but I had accidentally turned my phone to silent mode instead of setting the alarm, which is why I didn't receive Sue's phone calls at 1 AM, 2 AM, 2:30 AM, and so on. Finally, at around 8 AM, Roger woke me up and said, "You need to call Sue. She's been trying to get ahold of you."

Still in a sleepy stupor, I tried to process what was happening. "Why did Sue call you instead of me?" I asked Roger.

"Apparently your phone is dead or something," he said. "All I know is, Sue found my number and called me, looking for you. You should call her right away."

When I grabbed my phone from the nightstand, I discovered why she had called Roger. I could see the numerous missed calls from Sue, so I knew something was up. Sue never called me on a hunt unless it was an emergency.

She picked up, and I could hear distress in her voice.

"What's going on?" I asked her.

"Babe, your mom passed away late last night."

I figured it had to be one of my parents, but that didn't make the news any less heartbreaking. No matter how bad our relationship had been, she was still my mom, and I still loved her.

"Listen, there's nothing you can do here right now," Sue said. "And you just got there. Why don't you stay and hunt, and I'll keep you posted on things here?"

"I can't do that," I objected.

"Seriously, you should just stay. You're already there," she said, trying to convince me. "Your brother and I can start making arrangements and handle things until you get back."

"OK," I said. "Thanks. I love you."

"Love you, too," Sue said. "And don't worry about anything. We've got this."

Sue was very convincing, but I already felt guilty, and we hadn't even gone hunting yet. Yet I owed it to the disabled hunter Sam and Roger to help with the hunt. After all, it was my responsibility. While out in the woods that day, Sam and I had one of those "divine appointment" kind of moments, though I was unaware of it at the time.

"You know, I wish I had become a prosthetist," I shared.

"Why don't you?" Sam asked. "It's not too late."

"Well, I'd have to go back to college...."

"If you're serious about it," Sam continued, "why don't you come and see me when we get back?"

And that was that. With everything else going on, I never gave it another thought. Later that day, I knew I had to talk to Sue. We had been out of phone range for several hours, so once I got a signal, I called her.

"Hey, how's everything going?" I asked.

There was a long pause.

"Sue, everything OK?"

"Cam...maybe you'd better catch the next flight home," she told me.

I didn't know exactly what was going on, but I could tell from the tone of her voice that she was overwhelmed, and she didn't get overwhelmed very often. I wasn't able to get a flight out of Del Rio until the next morning. Once I was on the plane, I tried to mentally prepare myself for the next few days. I knew they wouldn't be easy, and I knew I would have to be the strong one. The long flight gave me a chance to reminisce about my mom. I was sad that we had never been close, but Mom wasn't really close with anyone. Though a lot of people, if they'd been in my shoes, probably would've been angry, I wasn't mad that she hadn't been the "June Cleaver" or "Carol Brady" kind of mother I had always desired. I actually felt sorry for her because I think, deep down, she would've liked to have been a good mom and a caring grandma, but she just couldn't do it, for some reason.

I'll never forget the night I went to the emergency room for a shoulder injury. We went to the closest hospital, and it happened to be the one where Mom had worked for many years. As the attending nurse took my health history, she said, "Tribolet…you wouldn't happen to be related to Shirley Tribolet, would you?"

"Yeah, she's my Mom," I answered.

"Really?" the nurse said, smiling. "Well, I should have known. She talks about you all the time, and she is crazy about those grandkids. She always tells us about how much she loves keeping them at her house. She shows off their pictures all the time."

I couldn't believe what I was hearing. My mom had never kept our children at her house, and, as far as I knew, they'd never been at her house by themselves—ever. I remember looking at Sue and shaking my head.

At the same time, I wondered why she would lie about being a doting mom and grandma. And then, it finally made sense to me—she really wanted to be that kind of mom and grandma. But, since she had failed miserably at both, it was just easier to pretend that she was everything she had wanted to be, instead of facing up to the reality that she never could be.

Closure

Once I arrived home, I went into overdrive, making funeral arrangements and calling people to notify them of Mom's passing. Tracey, who had been closer to Mom than I had been, wasn't handling her death very well, and my sister hadn't yet arrived from D.C. We weren't even sure if my older brother would come. So, I was the obvious choice when it came to picking out her casket, writing her obituary, and handling other responsibilities.

Somehow, we all made it through her service and burial, but we still had the monumental task of cleaning out the house she'd shared with dad before their divorce a few years prior. Neither of my brothers wanted any part of that task, so my sister and her husband, as well as Braden and I, worked together to clean, sort, and store everything.

There were so many memories in that childhood home of ours, but none of them was good. As I cleaned out Mom's nightstand, I found her floral calendar book. You hardly ever saw her without it. It was like an old-fashioned BlackBerry to her, and she lived by it. I held it up to my nose.

Smells just like Mom's perfume, I thought.

As I opened it, a receipt fell to the floor. I picked it up and couldn't believe what I found. It was a receipt for a casket—my casket! I stopped breathing for a moment as I stared at that yellowed piece of paper. According to the receipt, the casket had been purchased in August 1986, right after the shooting. And along the side of the receipt, Mom had written down the names of the pallbearers who would serve at my funeral.

"Look at this," I said, handing it to Braden.

"Is that what I think it is?" he asked, visibly creeped out.

"Yeah, I think it is."

Of course, I knew I had died several times—thirteen, to be exact—over the course of those months in the hospital, but to see a receipt for my casket, to see it in writing, was a heavy dose of reality.

New Year, Same Situation

We had buried Mom, cleaned out her house, put it on the market in December, and managed to make it through the holidays without too much additional stress. I remember when the ball dropped that year and we welcomed 2011—I was very relieved. It's not that 2010 had been all bad, but the last part of it had been quite difficult, and I was ready to begin the New Year with new hope.

However, exactly thirty-one days after my mom died, I was awakened by a ringing telephone in the middle of the night. It was the nursing home.

"Mr. Tribolet?" said the voice on other end of the phone.

"Yes?"

"I'm calling about your father…he probably isn't going to make it through the night, and we thought you should know."

"Thank you," I managed. "We'll be right over."

Sue was already up and aware of what was going on, so we both threw on some clothes, told Braden the news without awaking Julia, and headed for the nursing home.

On the drive over, I tried so hard to think of the good times I had shared with my father, but they had been few and far between. In fact, just two days before, he had looked me right in the eyes and said, "I've always loved your sister more than you." That's just who he was, and no matter how hard I tried, I couldn't make him love me.

When we arrived, Dad was still alive, but he was nonresponsive. Sue and I were the first ones there, so we took that time to pray for him, hoping he could hear us and agree with us. We had tried so many times before to share Jesus with Dad, but he would always say, "I don't believe in heaven or hell, and I don't want to hear any more about it."

He was a little kinder to Sue when she spoke about God, but whenever I tried to share my testimony and tell him about the visions I'd had of both heaven and hell, he would say, "You were on morphine, that's all. It wasn't real. Now, shut up."

But I knew it was real, and I didn't want Dad to go to hell. I really hoped that he could hear us. I wanted to believe that he was praying silently, right along with us, but I could never know for sure. Dad passed just after sunrise.

Unlike Mom, Dad had prearranged his funeral. He didn't want a service, and he wanted to be cremated. Honoring his wishes, my dad's brother and I met at the funeral home to sign off on everything. We said our good-byes, and that was it.

More Loss

Just when I thought it couldn't get any worse, it did. The day my father died, the fire sprinkler installation company I worked for was flying people into Fort Wayne to fire me. I was out of the office that day, so they came back the following Wednesday to let me go. They didn't even offer any severance pay, since I had received a bonus before Christmas. All I received was a "Thank you very much, but your services are no longer required here."

I drove home feeling pretty numb. Both of my parents had died, and we were still paying off their services and burials, because neither one of them had life insurance. And then I had lost my job. If someone had run over my dog, I would've been living the lyrics of a bad country song.

When I walked in the door, Sue was already home. She was buzzing about the kitchen, and the kids were doing homework in the living room. As I looked at my sweet family, I felt like a failure.

How am I going to support them? Who will hire me? I thought.

"Hey, want some supper?" Sue said from the kitchen.

"Don't really have an appetite."

"What's wrong?" she asked. "Are you getting sick?"

"Sue, I lost my job today."

"You're kidding," she said. "I can't believe it! Do they know that you just buried both of your parents?"

"I don't think corporate really cares about my personal life too much," I said. "Anyway, it's over. I'm done."

Sue didn't say anything right away, but I could tell she was stewing. She had that whole righteous anger thing going on, so I just plopped down on the couch, ready to spend the rest of the night sulking.

Then, after a bit, she joined me on the couch.

"OK, here's what we're going to do," she said, in her Polly Positive voice. "I will pick up some extra hours at work, and you can spend some time figuring out what exactly you want to do. Maybe you should go back to school…have you thought about that?"

Actually, I hadn't thought about it. In that moment, memories of my conversation with Sam from SRT came flooding back. I told Sue about the brief conversation I'd had with him in Texas, and she encouraged me to go see him.

So I did.

When I met with him at his office, he encouraged me to finish my business degree. Then he said, "If you're going to represent me and SRT, I'm getting you new legs."

I was overwhelmed, scared, and excited at the same time. As bad as life had been over the past month, I still believed that God had a plan for my life. I had to remind myself of that daily, but I knew He hadn't given up on me, and I couldn't give up, either. After all, that had been my life motto for many years, and I couldn't let the loss of my parents and my job make me a quitter.

That month, I enrolled in online classes and also began remodeling our master bathroom. I'd always been a carpenter, and since I would be at home until I could find work, I thought, *What better time to remodel our bathroom? It will make Sue happy, and it will keep me busy.*

One day, while I was crafting our bathroom cabinetry, I got a call from the president of another fire sprinkler installation company in the area. He said he had heard I'd lost my job with his competitor, and he wondered if I would come to work for him.

"Here's the thing," I confessed. "I just enrolled in online classes that begin in March. I want to finish my bachelor's degree in business administration. It's important to me."

"I admire that," he said. "But you could do your class work at night and work for me during the day, couldn't you?"

"Absolutely."

"Good, then it's all set," he said. "Come in on Monday, and we'll discuss all the details, and you'll have to do all that HR paperwork. Welcome aboard, Cam."

"Thanks," I said, stunned at what had just transpired. "See you soon."

It was lucky I was almost through with the bathroom, because I would be going back to work as a senior engineer technician on Monday. It had been a month of ups and downs, but God had been faithful through it all—even on the days when I couldn't feel Him. He had been working behind the scenes on my behalf, and now I had a new job, a newly remodeled bathroom, a new educational opportunity, new legs, and a new outlook on my future. The New Year was looking up.

TWELVE

THE CLIMB

Cam, I just watched your story on TV. You really touched my heart. Your journey and how you have overcome so much adversity is truly amazing! I think everyone goes through the 'Why me, Lord?' at some point in his or her life. You've been blessed to get the answer to that question. Keep up the good fight and the awesome work!

God bless,

Don

Cam, I just watched your program on the Sportsman Channel. I was just flipping through the channels and saw you telling your story. You brought me to tears. You are THE MAN! I don't know you, but I am a better person just for listening to your story.

Thank you so much.

David

As I read through the morning's e-mails, I was humbled. Our television show, *The Way Outfitters Adventures*, had debuted in December 2011, and the feedback I had received was tremendous. Every day, it seemed that someone else had watched our premiere episode, on which I share my story, and I'd receive another e-mail telling me to keep doing what I was doing, that I was an inspiration, and that I was making a difference. Wow. If someone would've told me, back when I was a little boy sneaking alcohol from my parents' bar so that I could get drunk and escape my miserable existence, that I'd be an inspiration, I wouldn't have believed him. And if someone would've told me, back when I was prostituting myself to get another hit of cocaine, that I would make a difference in someone's life, I certainly wouldn't have believed him. But that's why it's called a testimony, I guess. All of these great tests in my life have resulted in an even greater test-imony. And, the amazing thing was, people wanted to hear it.

At this point in my life, I had already been written about in my local newspaper, as well as in *Buckmasters Whitetail Magazine* and *InMotion* magazine, and featured on the television program *I Survived…Beyond and Back* on the Biography Channel. In addition, I'd been in a national TV commercial for BraunAbility, as well as featured in a national ad campaign for SRT Prosthetics & Orthotics. I'd spoken at multiple fund-raising banquets for Buckmasters, as well as given my testimony to church congregations, youth groups, Boy Scout troops, sports organizations, and many other groups. As important as all of that was, and as honored as I felt to do those things, being on *The Way Outfitters Adventures* was somehow different. I had already discovered that I was born to help people, and now I had the perfect platform from which to do it. Sharing my story on the first episode of *The Way Outfitters Adventures* was liberating. To look into the camera and tell viewers that there is life after amputation and that disabilities do not have to define them was very emotional for me. I put my story out there to be judged and evaluated. The old me would've found that uncomfortable and vulnerable, but the new me—the me that had been evolving since I'd given my life to God in 2004—felt empowered and purposeful.

As I read through those e-mails again, I remembered the prayer that the men at Promise Keepers had prayed over me years before, and I thanked God that He was answering that prayer and allowing me to be used by Him for His glory. Not only was I getting to share my story with the world, but, as program host, I also was being given an incredible opportunity to share other people's stories of triumph over tragedy. Whether I'm featuring a terminally ill child whose dream is to go on a deer hunt in West Texas or chatting with a disabled veteran while fishing for sharks down in Key West, each story is motivating and uplifting, and these brave people make me want to be better, grow stronger, and do more. At the time of this writing, we have filmed thirteen episodes, and the show has been nominated for three industry awards.

Who knows where God will take *The Way Outfitters Adventures?* All I know is that there are more stories to tell, more people to inspire, and more hunts to plan and participate in. Of course, not all of The Way Outfitters' hunts are able to be featured on the TV program; nevertheless, all are inspiring. So far, we have taken more than one hundred guests facing serious challenges on three-day adventures across the United States. It's the most rewarding work I've ever done. Raising funds for this charity is challenging, at times, but I've never met a challenge I didn't like.

I think that's why I'm always pushing myself to try new things. It's like I'm checking items off on my imaginary bucket list (because I don't really have one written down anywhere). Downhill monoskiing: check. Handbiking: check. Skeet shooting: check. Snowmobiling: check. Bungee jumping: check. Parasailing: check. Jet-skiing: check. Kneeboarding: check. Swimming: check. Climbing to the top of a mountain...not yet.

Mountaintop Experience

Climbing a mountain was next on the agenda; I just didn't know it until the summer of 2012. That's when a man contacted The Way Outfitters, looking for a disabled sportsman who might be interested in participating in a mountain climb in California the following year. He explained that he needed just one more person to complete his team of ten. I was immediately interested and told him my background. Moments later, I had made the cut! I was in! He said he planned to film the climb for a TV special, and I couldn't wait. The mountain of choice, he explained, was Mount Whitney in California—the highest mountain in the United States.

The more he talked about the climb, the more excited I became. But, as the months passed, the climb kept getting postponed, and that worried me. Then I got word that he was backing out of the entire Mount Whitney adventure. His plans to film it for TV had hit a roadblock, and he e-mailed to say that he had to cancel the climb.

"I still want to do it," I told Sue one night during dinner.

"Then why don't you?" she said.

"I just might. Cost would be the stopper. I'll have to do some research."

With Braden a freshman in college, I wanted to be responsible with our funds, but it was worth looking into. I called a mountain guide in California and asked about the possibility of hiring him for a three-day climb in July 2013. He gave me a quote and explained that we would hike on the first day to the base camp—an elevation of about 10,000 feet—and then head for the 14,000-foot summit on day two. On day three, we would journey back down the mountain. When I told him I was disabled, he didn't seem a bit surprised or worried.

"Are you training for the climb?" he asked.

"Of course," I said, even though I hadn't done much yet.

At the end of our phone call, the mountain climb seemed like more of a possibility, but I really didn't want to do it by myself. However, I didn't want to ask Sue to accompany me and make her feel obligated to do so, especially if she didn't want to go. That night, while relaxing on the couch, I told Sue about the guide and the details of the climb.

"So, would it be a lot more money if I came along?" she asked.

"Do you want to go with me? Because I really want you to go, but I didn't want you to feel obligated."

"I think I'd like to go," she said.

Once Sue was in, I kicked into full gear with our planning. We booked our flights to Las Vegas and made preparations to rent a car to drive to the base of Mount Whitney. Now we just had to prepare for the climb. I stopped by the local Anytime Fitness to inquire about trainers and to see if I could take over Braden's membership, since he was away at college.

Looking at my "robot legs," as my kids like to call them, the young man at the front asked what kind of training I needed.

"Well, I am training to climb Mount Whitney in California, which is a three-day climb," I explained, "so I really need to work on my upper-body strength and core training, as well as cardiovascular, of course."

"Wait just a minute," he said. "I want to ask my manager something."

When I met the manager, he was excited about getting involved in my training and offered me a free membership. I thanked him and asked if they had any student trainers or someone I could hire to get me in shape for such a feat, and the favor continued.

"We have several trainers," he answered. "And how about if I pick up half of your trainer's fee?"

"That would be amazing," I said, then proceeded to tell him the whole story of how the idea for the climb had originally came about and how we were doing it on our own now.

My training began that day, and Sue and I also started walking five miles together several days a week.

It seemed that everywhere I went, people wanted to get involved and help me make this climb a reality. When I discussed the climb with Sam at SRT, he said that I'd need different legs and offered to make them for me. Then, Endolite prosthetics donated new Echelon feet for the climb—on one condition. They requested that I send a picture of my donated Echelon feet on top of the mountain, which I agreed to do.

I was so excited about what God was doing that I found myself talking about it to anyone who would listen. On one particular day, that person happened to be my phlebotomist at Parkview Hospital. While she took my blood, I told her all about the upcoming climb.

"I think that is amazing, Cam," she said.

It turned out that she thought it was so amazing, she told the president of Parkview Hospital all about it, and he sent me an e-mail saying he wanted to meet. God just kept opening doors, and I just kept walking through them—one robot leg at a time. At the end of my meeting with the president of Parkview Hospital, I had an official sponsor for the climb—he'd covered almost 90 percent of the overall expense. I had been so nervous to step out and go for it, afraid it would cost too much and take money away from Braden's college fund, but God had a plan all along.

Of all the adventures I have experienced and the challenges I have sought out, the mountain climb was the hardest thing I ever attempted. If it wasn't for my Anytime Fitness trainer, Jessica Fuller, I am positive that I would not have made it as far as I did. On the first day of the trip, Sue and I, along with our climbing guide, Neil Woodruff from SWS Mountain Guides, began our ascent up the Mount Whitney Trail. The terrain started simply enough—a good one-mile hike upward, which got our hearts pumping and our excitement level up. Then we reached the Mountaineers Route, and I saw for the first time how difficult this climb was going to be. What was above us was boulder after boulder and a small foot trail that would eventually lead us up to an elevation of 14,500 feet. However, the mountain and my disability clashed—and the mountain won. At an elevation of nearly 10,000 feet, a series of ledges stopped me from my quest of reaching the summit. Yet another roadblock had been put in front of me. But I'm not one to give up easily.

Two days later, after climbing for nearly twelve hours straight on the first day of our trip to attempt Mount Whitney, we changed our strategy and moved to another mountain to conquer. A mountaintop near Mount Langley proved to be yet another challenge that tested my strength and endurance and pushed my disability to its limits. After traversing cliff ledges that were only about twelve inches wide, and after nearly twelve hours of climbing, we were finally back at the base of the mountain. I couldn't help but look up in awe at what I had finally accomplished.

On the last day of the trip, we were met with a surprise from our guide, Neil. I had mentioned to Neil that I had always wanted to learn to rappel, so he took us to the Alabama Hills Mountain Range for some one-on-one ascending and rappelling training. Sue, on the other hand, didn't share my crazy enthusiasm for hanging from a rope a hundred feet in the air, so she manned the camera as I prepared to head upward. After several failed attempts, Neil was able to calculate the correct method of attachment that I needed in order for my center of gravity to be positioned correctly on the rock face. Within minutes, I was scaling a rock face! The view was beautiful and breathtaking; the sun was low on the horizon, and shadows of the mountain range made interesting alien-like shapes on the desert floor. I could see Sue at the bottom and heard her cheering as I perched on the top of that rock face. Reluctantly, I held on to the rope with one hand and thrust my fist in the air in triumph before I quickly grabbed the rope again.

What a trip. Not only did I set out to do what I wanted to do, but I was able to share all of this with my wife as we celebrated our twenty-fifth anniversary on a mountain. In a way, the climb symbolized my entire life, as well as the life that Sue and I share. Life is an uphill battle, a daily challenge to move forward and excel. But God has always prepared us and kept us focused—He is faithful to get us ready for the next challenge. Sue made an observation that I hadn't considered until we were coming off the mountain. She looked at me and said, "It just hit me that after twenty-five years of marriage, this is the first time that we actually went for a walk."

Since that time, Braden and I decided that the best way to celebrate my successful climb and the many goals that he had achieved in recent years was to get matching tattoos across our backs that say, "Never Give Up!" It's more than just an expression to us; it's become a part of us. It's the way we live our lives, and it will always be that way.

THIRTEEN

WHO IS DISABLED?

Whenever I hear a traffic report about a disabled car on the side of the road, I think to myself, *I wish they would use another word besides "disabled." Maybe "stalled," but not "disabled."* What the traffic reporter is saying is, "There is a car broken down, sitting on the side of the road, not moving." If that's the true definition of *disabled*, then don't call me disabled, because I am not sitting on the roadside of life, broken down, not moving. In fact, I am constantly moving, reaching new goals, accomplishing feats I once thought impossible, and living my life full-out. I guess that's why I don't like the labels that come with being an amputee—"disabled," "handicapped," "physically challenged," and so on. I always jokingly say, "I'm just like everybody else. I put my pants on one leg at a time, after I put my legs on one at a time."

In fact, I joke around a lot concerning my lack of legs. For instance, when people ask how tall I am, I always respond, "I am height adjustable," which is both funny and factual. If I'm wearing my legs, I'm quite tall. If I am on my stumps, I am about the height of Dorf on *The Carol Burnett Show*. I guess I just don't take myself too seriously, which is why I can joke around about my situation; but not everyone gets my sense of humor.

I'll never forget the time when Sue and I were eating at this wonderful buffet restaurant. Noticing the stack of plates piled next to me from repeat visits to the buffet, our server said, "Wow, you must have a hollow leg." Without missing a beat, I said, "Actually, I have two." He wasn't sure how to respond, but Sue and I had a good laugh.

I guess I do have a laugh at others' expense once in a while, but I don't do it to be cruel. For example, sometimes when I'm doing an on-the-job inspection, a client will notice that I'm using a cane and limping a bit, and ask, "What happened to your knee?" I usually tap my legs with my cane and say, "Well, I don't have any knees." Of course, the client is usually horrified and begins to apologize profusely, but I think it's kind of funny. I just try to break the ice and make the other person feel less threatened by my lack of legs.

When you live with a disability, you have to find the humor in life and make the best out of everything—especially doctor visits, because there are so many. Over the years, I have become great friends with the folks at my orthopedic doctor's office. In fact, the nurses there have nicknamed themselves "Cam's Posse." They always give me lots of hugs when I show up for my appointments, and sometimes they give me the comic relief I need, as well. One time, I was scheduled to see Dr. Pritchard about a shoulder replacement, but the nurse just assumed I was there about my legs—or what was left of them. She said, "OK, Cam, take your pants off, and the doctor will be with you in a moment." Before I could say anything, she caught her mistake, turned three shades of red, and said, "Never mind." We all had a good laugh. The Bible says, *"If you are cheerful, you feel good; if you are sad, you hurt all over"* (Proverbs 17:22 CEV), so I choose to laugh every day. And I choose to look at the bright side of life. That's one of the main messages I share when I speak to various church groups, disabled hunters, youth organizations, and so on.

I want to share with you a few more tidbits of wisdom that I've learned along the way—truths that have kept me pushing on when I wanted to quit; truths that have been road tested and approved.

Tidbits of Wisdom

1. Don't let your circumstances define you.

When people look at me, I want them to look past my prosthetic legs and see Cam. I want them to know that I am not defined by my lack of legs. Sure, the injuries and eventual amputations played a part in shaping who I have become, but they're not the only thing that makes me who I am. In order to make others see that there is more to me than my disability, I try not to use my lack of legs as an excuse or to let it hinder me from doing something I want to do. In the same way, you should not make excuses for your circumstances or let them hinder you from doing what you want to do. Go for it—and never give up!

2. Get rid of the "I can't" mentality.

Sometimes, we can be our own worst enemies. We defeat ourselves in our minds by dwelling on the things we can't do instead of focusing on new ways of doing things. For example, I may not be able to downhill ski in the traditional manner, but I can go downhill monoskiing. Remove "I can't" from your vocabulary and begin each day believing that you can accomplish anything you set out to do. The Bible says, "*I can do all things through Christ who strengthens me*" (Philippians 4:13). When you start to feel discouraged and defeated, meditate on that verse and begin to see yourself as an overcomer.

3. Take time to appreciate life.

When I was on the ten-day African safari, I learned so much from our hunt guide, Rudy. Not only did he know the best places to hunt, but also he knew the best location to enjoy a breathtaking sunset. He taught me the importance of appreciating the beauty of this world and taking the time to enjoy it. Now, I get up a little earlier each morning and time my commute so that I get to see the sunrise on my way to work. I'm trying to live my life with this quote in mind: "Life is not measured by the number of breaths we take but by the moments that take our breath away." I believe if everyone adopted this same outlook, it would be a much happier, nicer, slower-paced world.

4. Never lose the competitive spirit.

Have you suffered a disability or been through a terrible divorce or battled an ongoing illness or suffered another kind of heartbreaking setback? Never let those negative circumstances rob you of your competitive spirit. There's something about a competitive spirit that drives a person to do better, go faster, climb higher, reach farther, and last longer. I've seen downtrodden guys undergo a complete turnaround once they get a gun in their hands and go out on a hunt.

Suddenly, whatever had died inside of them is revived, and that competitive spirit returns, so that they are more positive, joyful, and energetic. So, go fishing. Go hunting. Join a basketball league. Start a card club. Challenge your family to game of bowling next weekend. Challenge your children in some of their favorite video games (and be prepared to get your butt kicked). Do whatever you have to do, but reawaken your competitive spirit.

5. Be a giver, not a taker.

My family will tell you that I love doing nice things for them. I take great pleasure in surprising Sue with flowers, planning Daddy-daughter dates with Julia, and organizing weekend trips with Braden. I also try to do small things to let them know that I love them every single day, whether it be giving Sue a compliment or running Julia to the mall or sending Braden an encouraging text message.

My favorite thing to do for those I love is to plan elaborate celebrations and purchase special gifts. For example, Julia has always wanted to go to Disney World in Florida, and so, for her sixteenth birthday, the Tribolet family will be headed south to visit Mickey and Minnie and all the rest of the Disney characters. Sure, it will be an expensive trip, but we're already saving for that big birthday celebration, as it's still a couple of years off.

When I met a disabled craftsman who makes custom knives from antlers, I ordered one for my son, knowing how much he loves hunting knives. This master craftsman fashioned Braden's knife out of polished brass and buffalo horn with a Damascus blade. It's a gorgeous creation in black and gold, which are Braden's school's colors. Then, to make it even more personal, I asked the craftsman to engrave "Never give up" on one side of the knife and Romans 5:3–5 on the other. When I gave it to Braden for Christmas last year, he was visibly moved and said it was his favorite gift. Sure, I could've just given him some cash and said, "Buy what you want, Son," but I wanted him to know that I thought he was special and that I'd had a knife made that reflected his uniqueness. If I've learned anything from what I've been through, it's that you should value the people in your life and never assume that you'll have another day to show your love to them. Do it today!

6. Celebrate small achievements but set really big goals.

Bible teacher and author Joyce Meyer once said, "Enjoy where you are on the way to where you're going." I thought that was a very strong and sound teaching.

It certainly resonated with me. Part of enjoying where you are is taking time to celebrate your small achievements. Don't be in such a hurry to tackle the next goal that you forget to celebrate the one you just accomplished. Braden and I are getting the "Never Give Up" matching tattoos as a reward for achieving our latest goals. What will you do to celebrate your next victory? It might be something as simple as giving yourself a day off from work to do absolutely nothing; but whatever you choose, make sure you enjoy it. Then, get back on track and go for the next goal. Aim high! Go for the gold! Go big or go home! I also like what Les Brown once said: "Shoot for the moon. Even if you miss, you'll land among the stars."

7. Have an attitude of gratitude.

When Julia was about three years old, we went on a family vacation at a resort in Florida. One day, we spent the morning enjoying the pool, and as the lunch hour approached, we were getting pretty hungry.

"Sue, I'm going to take the kids back to the condo and grab something to eat," I said. "Do you want me to bring you anything back?"

"No, I'm fine—thanks," she answered, her nose buried in a book.

I climbed into my wheelchair and headed for the condo, with Braden and Julia walking right alongside me, but Julia wasn't paying attention. As I wheeled right, following the direction of the pool deck, Julia kept walking straight and fell into the deep end of the pool. Instinctively, I dove out of my wheelchair and into the water to save my baby girl. Julia was perfectly fine afterward, and kept saying, "Daddy saved me." For the entire rest of the trip, as well as for several months later, she would just randomly tell people, "Daddy saved me." Her little heart was so full of gratitude that it just oozed out of her. What a great way to live! I want to be like Julia and have so much gratitude in my heart that it just oozes out of me, until I'm telling everyone I encounter, "Daddy saved me." Because He did.

From Setbacks to Setups

Romans 5:3–5 has become a very special Scripture passage to me because it so aptly describes what I've been through and how I've made it through. It says,

And not only that, but we also glory in tribulations, knowing that tribulation produces perseverance; and perseverance, character; and character, hope. Now hope does not disappoint, because the love of God has been poured out in our hearts by the Holy Spirit who was given to us. (Romans 5:3–5)

In other words, the problems we encounter are not setbacks but rather setups for more of God in our lives. Who wouldn't want more perseverance, character, and hope? And who wouldn't want more of God's love? The trials I have encountered in life—growing up in a very dysfunctional home, getting shot in such a violent crime, dying and then being brought back to life, losing my legs, learning to walk again, going through the GIFT procedure to conceive Braden, waiting to adopt Julia, losing both of my parents and my job within a month, and on and on—were all very difficult. When people hear my testimony, I often get comments like, "Wow, you have been through so much; nothing has come easy for you." I always smile and say, "It does seem that way, doesn't it? But I wouldn't change one thing." That statement always floors people. It certainly surprised my dad when I said it to him.

Days before my father passed away, we actually had a real conversation—one that wasn't filled with profanity and insults. He looked at me with very sad eyes and said, "I've always felt responsible for your accident."

I tried to interrupt him, but he kept speaking.

"Let me finish," he said. "I feel like, as your father, I should've stepped in and stopped you from doing the destructive stuff you were doing, but I didn't."

"Dad, it wasn't your fault," I said, trying to comfort him. "It was my fault—all mine. I am the one who let this happen, and if I had the chance to do it all over again, I would."

He looked at me like I had lost my mind.

"I'm serious, Dad," I continued. "August thirty-first, nineteen eighty-six, was the best day of my life, because that was the day I got a second chance…the day I became a better man."

I'm not sure that Dad ever really understood what I was saying, but I'm hoping you do. See, I feel like God has blessed me, along with others who have gone through hardships, with a very special gift—the strength to fight adversity and a testimony to inspire others.

Maybe you've gone through hardships, or maybe you're still in the fight. I want to encourage you to stay strong and realize that you've been given those same gifts. Embrace your new beginning, and don't ever give up! Someday, you'll look back on your struggles and, like me, be able to say, "I would not change one thing, because every adversity I've overcome has been a gift from God and has shaped the person I have become."

I recently received an e-mail from a man who saw my story on TV. He wrote:

Your story really inspired me. As a fellow amputee, I figure if you can do what you're doing, I can do more with my life. I'm tired of limitations. I'm tired of living how I'm living. I want to be unstoppable. And today, I have made the decision to be just that—unstoppable.

Me, too.

AFTERWORD

DIVINE DIRECTION

Losing my legs turned out to be an unexpected gift. Twenty-six years after my accident, I know that things don't just happen in life. Everything is preplanned if you'll just let Jesus lead you. I firmly believe that God has made bricks with my name on them and has paved a road for me to follow. Have I always followed that path? No, but I am following it now, because I know that it leads to peace, contentment, and total fulfillment.

You see, I believe I was supposed to get shot that night in 1986. I believe I was supposed to meet my wife in the hospital. I believe we were supposed to have two beautiful children. I believe I was supposed to work with other disabled individuals and inspire them. And I believe I was supposed to write this book and share my story with others. Not only that, but I know that you were supposed to pick up my book today, or you wouldn't be reading these words right now.

God sets up divine appointments for us throughout our lives. We may not always recognize them, but they are there. I am a walking miracle. I am a living testimony of God's faithfulness and resurrection power. And I'm here to tell you that miracles do happen, if you'll just give God control of your heart and life.

Now, does that mean everything is going to be easy in life? Having undergone more than thirty operations, I can answer "Definitely not." What happens when you give God control is that He walks with you as you journey down His path for your life. He will be there to help you up when you stumble, and He will carry you when you can't walk anymore. He is a faithful God—I speak from experience. When I say that I've been there, I speak honestly. I have been a drug addict and have battled alcohol dependency. I have contemplated suicide more than once. I have endured more physical pain than any human should have to go through. I have died thirteen different times and stared the devil in the face. I have seen the light and experienced Jesus up close and personal. I have been rejected by those I loved the most. I have lost everything and had to start over. And, through all that, I've seen God turn it all around for His glory and my gain.

This is my story—my new beginning—my chance to learn to live again after dying. I hope you'll embark on the same journey.

ABOUT THE AUTHOR

Cam Tribolet is many things—a living miracle, an amputee, a husband and father, a public speaker, a TV personality, a hunter, a skier, a volunteer, an architectural engineer, and a man with an amazing story. After his tragedy and amazing recovery, Cam began a support group for amputees and often speaks to new amputees about his experiences, encouraging them to move forward and embrace their new lives. A gifted public speaker, Cam shares his testimony of courage and strength every year with Boy Scout troops, church congregations, youth groups, convention attendees, occupational therapy students, and other large groups. Winner of the 2008 Pathfinder Award from Safari Club International for his volunteer work with the disabled community, Cam continues to let his light shine on everyone he personally encounters. His moving story was featured in *I Survived...Beyond and Back* on the Biography Channel. Cam lives with his wife, Sue, and their two children, Braden and Julia, in Fort Wayne, Indiana.